Campbell's

CREATIVE COOKING
WITH SOUP

Campbell's

CREATIVE COOKING
WITH SOUP

BEEKMAN HOUSE
New York

© 1985 Campbell Soup Company

"Campbell's" and "V-8" are registered trademarks of Campbell Soup Company.

This book was prepared by the Publications Center of Campbell Soup Company, Camden, NJ 08101. Betty Cronin, Director; Flora Szatkowski, Editor; Patrícia A. Ward and Elaine Gagliardi, Home Economists. Photographer, William R. Houssell; Food Stylist, Marianne Langan; and Accessories Stylist, Lynn Wilson.

Library of Congress Catalog Card Number: 84-62149

ISBN: 0-517-45250-2

This edition published by:
Beekman House
Distributed by Crown Publishers, Inc.
One Park Avenue
New York, New York 10016

Manufactured in the United States of America
10 9 8 7 6 5 4 3 2 1

Contents

Cooking with Soup... Your Way

Did you ever wish someone would write a cookbook just for you? Someone has, and it's different from any other cookbook you've ever used. That's because it's planned for flexibility—to help you with your busy schedule, your family's tastes, your budget, your food supplies, even your creativity.

Each recipe includes a unique chart that shows you how to vary ingredients to suit your needs. For example, if a recipe suggests peas and you don't like peas, you can use another alternative—possibly corn or spinach. If you're all out of cream of mushroom soup, the recipe might suggest using cream of celery or another soup. Or, if your budget favors tuna over shrimp, you can take that option.

These variations make every recipe a springboard to as many as 256 different dishes, for a total of more than 19,000 combinations in the book. You're sure to find plenty of ways to make everyday meals special and special meals extraordinary.

The secret to making these recipes so versatile is the magic of canned soup. Cream-style soups start a foolproof sauce for dishes that require one; broth-based soups add a blend of seasonings to foods cooked with liquid.

If you're a beginning cook, you'll appreciate the simplicity of recipes made with soup. If you're more experienced, you'll enjoy the versatility of using soup to create your own new recipes.

You're already familiar with soup as a good old-fashioned food, but soup is also very contemporary. It goes into pasta and pizza, quiche and kabobs, tacos and stir-frys, even vegetarian main dishes. Besides these tempting entrées are fresh salads, full-flavored appetizers, hearty soups, even delicious desserts.

You can use these recipes with confidence because they have been carefully tested in Campbell's kitchens. Each variation has been created to work well with every other ingredient combination on the chart. Once you start using the recipes, you'll find your own favorites and you'll see how well they fit into your busy lifestyle. Yes, this book really is written for you!

How to Use This Book

Each recipe in this book consists of three parts: an ingredient list, a chart and preparation instructions.

Souper Easy Quiche

4 eggs
1 can (10¾ to 11 ounces) condensed **Soup**
½ cup light cream
1 cup shredded **Cheese**
Meat
½ cup **Vegetable**
1 9-inch unbaked piecrust
Ground nutmeg

} Ingredient List

Soup	Cheese	Meat	Vegetable
Cheddar cheese	sharp Cheddar	½ cup diced cooked ham	drained, cooked chopped broccoli
cream of mushroom	American	6 slices bacon, cooked, drained and crumbled	drained, cooked cut asparagus
cream of onion	Monterey Jack	½ cup diced cooked chicken	sliced mushrooms
cream of celery	Swiss	½ cup diced cooked turkey	drained, cooked chopped spinach

} Chart

1. In medium bowl, beat eggs until foamy. Gradually add **Soup** and cream, mixing well.

2. Sprinkle **Cheese, Meat** and **Vegetable** evenly over piecrust. Pour soup mixture over all. Sprinkle with nutmeg.

3. Bake at 350°F. 50 minutes or until center is set. Let stand 10 minutes before serving. Makes 6 servings.

} Preparation Instructions

Simply read the ingredient list as you would a normal recipe. When you come to an ingredient in **bold** type, refer to the chart. Choose from one of the options listed below the heading. For example, for 1 can condensed **Soup**, look under the heading "**Soup**" and choose from Cheddar cheese soup, cream of mushroom, cream of onion and cream of celery.

There are 2 ways to use this chart. You may choose all the items from a single horizontal row as indicated in red or you may skip around as indicated in green.

Once you have made all your selections, just follow the numbered steps.

That's all there is to it! You'll be preparing new recipes in no time.

Good Nutrition Can Be Your Way Too

Today's Americans are becoming more and more interested in the quality and nutrition of the foods they eat. They are learning that good food habits are essential to health and a general feeling of well-being. We at Campbell's are excited about this trend. We believe that good food contributes greatly to the quality of life.

One of the easiest ways to balance your diet is to eat a wide variety of foods. Each single food has something important to contribute to your health, but it takes a combination of foods to complete the nutritional balance.

That's how this book fits into your plan for good eating. With the wide choice of ingredients in each recipe chart, you can easily vary your diet according to your nutritional needs and tastes.

Like many other health-conscious consumers, you may be concerned about calories and sodium in the foods you eat. For that reason, we have calculated the amounts of sodium and calories in each recipe. Look for this information at the end of each chapter.

Because of space limitations, we are not able to provide figures for all of the possible combinations in the book. Instead, we have analyzed the horizontal rows of the charts. If you decide to use a different combination, these numbers can be a guide to your own choices.

Calorie and sodium figures are given for a single serving of a food. In some cases where you determine the amount of a recipe you use (notably sauces, salad dressings and dips), the calculations are for 1 tablespoon of the food.

For many of our recipes, we have included serving suggestions in the charts, such as accompaniments, dippers and garnishes. When no specific quantity is given for these, they are not included in the calorie and sodium values.

Sodium and calorie contents were calculated using computer based information from the Michigan State University database, Campbell Soup Company database and the United States Department of Agriculture.

Recipe Helps

Preheating the oven is unnecessary unless we tell you to do so. If your oven manufacturer recommends preheating the broiler, follow those directions.

1 soup can equals about 1¼ cups liquid.

Flour is measured by spooning lightly into a dry measure, then leveling off; sifting is not necessary.

Herbs are always dried unless a fresh herb is specified.

Light cream and half-and-half can be used interchangeably.

When green peppers are specified, use bell peppers, not chilies.

Campbell's

CREATIVE COOKING
WITH SOUP

Appetizers

⚜

Appetizer Cheesecake

2 tablespoons butter or margarine
1 cup zwieback crumbs
1 can (10¾ to 11 ounces) condensed **Soup**
1 container (15 ounces) ricotta cheese
2 packages (8 ounces each) cream cheese, softened
Cheese
2 eggs
1 clove garlic, minced
Seasoning
1 cup sour cream
Topper

Soup	Cheese	Seasoning	Topper
cream of celery	1 cup grated Romano	¼ teaspoon thyme leaves, crushed	caviar and sieved hard-cooked egg yolk
Cheddar cheese	1½ cups shredded Cheddar	3 tablespoons chopped fresh chives	sliced cucumber, green onion and fresh dill sprigs
tomato	1½ cups shredded Swiss	½ teaspoon basil leaves, crushed	tomato roses and green onion tops
cream of chicken	1½ cups shredded Muenster	1 teaspoon curry powder	chutney

1. In small saucepan over medium heat, melt butter; stir in crumbs. Press mixture firmly onto bottom of 9-inch springform pan.

2. In food processor or large bowl, combine **Soup,** ricotta cheese and cream cheese. Process with food processor or beat with electric mixer until smooth. Add **Cheese,** eggs, garlic and **Seasoning.** Beat until smooth. Turn into prepared pan and place in jelly-roll pan.

3. Bake at 325°F. 1½ hours or until puffy and lightly browned. Cool completely in pan on wire rack. Cover; refrigerate until serving time, at least 2 hours.

4. Spread sour cream over cake; garnish with **Topper.** Makes 16 appetizer servings.

Caponata

½ cup olive oil
1 medium eggplant, cut into ½-inch cubes
1 medium onion, sliced and separated into rings
½ cup **Vegetable**
1 clove garlic, minced
1 can (10½ to 11 ounces) condensed **Soup**
1 small bay leaf
½ teaspoon **Herb,** crushed
Flavoring
1½ teaspoons vinegar

Vegetable	Soup	Herb	Flavoring
sliced celery	tomato	thyme leaves	½ cup sliced pitted ripe olives
chopped green pepper	tomato bisque	marjoram leaves	½ cup sliced pimento-stuffed olives
diced Jerusalem artichokes	Spanish style vegetable	basil leaves	1 can (4 ounces) chopped green chilies, drained
chopped mushrooms	tomato rice	oregano leaves	½ cup chopped drained, cooked artichoke hearts

1. In 4-quart Dutch oven over medium heat, in hot oil, cook eggplant, onion, **Vegetable** and garlic 10 minutes or until onion is tender.

2. Stir in **Soup,** bay leaf and **Herb.** Reduce heat to low. Cover; simmer 15 minutes or until eggplant is tender. Remove from heat. Discard bay leaf.

3. Stir in **Flavoring** and vinegar. Serve hot or cold with crusty bread. Makes about 4 cups.

Tip: *Caponata improves in flavor after chilling overnight, whether you serve it hot or cold.*

To Microwave: Use ingredients as above but reduce oil to ¼ cup. In 3-quart microwave-safe casserole, combine only ¼ cup oil, eggplant, onion, **Vegetable** and garlic; cover. Microwave on HIGH 6 to 8 minutes until onion is tender and eggplant is translucent, stirring occasionally. Stir in **Soup,** bay leaf and **Herb;** cover. Microwave on HIGH 6 to 8 minutes until eggplant is tender, stirring occasionally. Discard bay leaf. Proceed as in Step 3.

Avocado Dip

1 can (10½ to 10¾ ounces) condensed **Soup**
1 package (8 ounces) cream cheese, softened
Seasoning 1
Seasoning 2
1 ripe avocado, peeled and seeded
Dipper

Soup	Seasoning 1	Seasoning 2	Dipper
cream of celery	1 tablespoon finely chopped onion	1 tablespoon chili powder	tortilla chips
cream of shrimp	1 tablespoon finely chopped shallots	2 teaspoons finely chopped, seeded jalapeño peppers	thinly sliced bagels, toasted
cream of chicken	1 clove garlic, minced	¼ teaspoon hot pepper sauce	assorted raw vegetables

1. In medium bowl with mixer at low speed, gradually beat **Soup** into cream cheese until smooth. Beat in **Seasoning 1** and **Seasoning 2**.

2. Mash avocado; beat into soup mixture. Serve with **Dipper**. Makes about 2 cups.

Mexican-Style Appetizer

1 can (11½ ounces) condensed bean with bacon soup
1 package (1¼ ounces) taco seasoning mix
¼ teaspoon hot pepper sauce
1 cup sour cream
1 can (4 ounces) chopped green chilies, drained
½ cup **Flavoring**
1 cup shredded **Cheese**
½ cup **Topper**
½ cup chopped tomato
Dipper

Flavoring	Cheese	Topper	Dipper
sliced pimento-stuffed olives	longhorn	alfalfa sprouts	tortilla chips
diced cooked ham	Monterey Jack	chopped green pepper	pita bread, torn and toasted
diced avocado	Cheddar	shredded lettuce	celery sticks
diced pepperoni	mozzarella	chopped celery with leaves	sliced jícama

1. In small bowl, combine soup with taco seasoning mix and hot pepper sauce; stir until blended. On large serving plate, spread mixture into a 6-inch round. Spread sides and top of bean mixture with sour cream to cover.

2. Layer chilies, **Flavoring, Cheese, Topper** and tomato over sour cream. Cover; refrigerate until serving time, at least 4 hours. Surround with **Dipper.** Makes 10 appetizer servings.

Snappy Cocktail Dip

1 can (10½ to 10¾ ounces) condensed **Soup**
1 package (8 ounces) cream cheese, softened
Seafood
2 tablespoons chopped fresh parsley
2 tablespoons finely chopped onion
Seasoning
Dipper

Soup	Seafood	Seasoning	Dipper
cream of celery	1 can (7¾ ounces) salmon, drained and flaked	¼ teaspoon hot pepper sauce	assorted raw vegetables
cream of mushroom	1 can (6½ ounces) minced clams, drained	2 teaspoons prepared spicy brown mustard	potato chips
cream of chicken	1 can (7 ounces) crab meat, drained, picked over and flaked	1 tablespoon lemon juice	melba toast
golden mushroom	1 can (about 7 ounces) tuna, drained and flaked	2 teaspoons prepared horseradish	crackers

1. In medium bowl with mixer at low speed, beat **Soup** into cream cheese just until blended.

2. Stir in **Seafood,** parsley, onion and **Seasoning,** mixing well. Cover; refrigerate until serving time, at least 4 hours. Serve with **Dipper.** Makes about 2¾ cups.

Cheese Ball

1 can (11¼ to 11½ ounces) condensed **Soup**
¼ cup salsa
3 cups shredded **Cheese**
Seasoning
Coating
Assorted crackers

Soup	Cheese	Seasoning	Coating
bean with bacon	sharp Cheddar	1 clove garlic, minced	chopped fresh parsley
chili beef	Monterey Jack	½ teaspoon hot pepper sauce	finely crushed corn chips
split pea with ham and bacon	American	½ teaspoon dry mustard	chopped walnuts

1. In medium bowl with mixer at low speed or in food processor, beat or process **Soup,** salsa, **Cheese** and **Seasoning** until as smooth as possible. Cover and chill 4 hours or overnight.

2. On waxed paper, place **Coating.** Shape cheese mixture into ball and roll in coating until well covered. Serve with crackers. Makes 1 ball, 16 appetizer servings.

Cheese-Stuffed Vegetables

1 can (10½ to 10¾ ounces) condensed **Soup**
1 package (8 ounces) cream cheese, softened
1 to 2 tablespoons lemon juice
1 clove garlic, minced
½ teaspoon **Herb,** crushed
¼ teaspoon **Spice**
Vegetables
Chopped fresh parsley

Soup	Herb	Spice	Vegetables
cream of onion	summer savory leaves	pepper	cherry tomatoes, tops and centers removed
cream of celery	tarragon leaves	ground nutmeg	celery stalks, cut into 2-inch pieces
cream of mushroom	thyme leaves	paprika	snow pea pods, cut open

1. In medium bowl with mixer at low speed, beat **Soup** into cream cheese until well blended. Beat in lemon juice, garlic, **Herb** and **Spice.** Cover; refrigerate until serving time, at least 4 hours.

2. Using a spoon or decorating tube, stuff cheese mixture into **Vegetables.** Sprinkle with parsley. Makes about 2¼ cups filling, 36 appetizers.

Tip: *Use cheese mixture as a spread; chill and serve with crackers.*

Tomato Cheese Fondue

2 tablespoons butter or margarine
1 cup chopped tomatoes
½ cup chopped onion
1 clove garlic, minced
1 can (10¾ to 11 ounces) condensed **Soup**
Seasoning
Cheese, shredded
Dipper

Soup	Seasoning	Cheese	Dipper
cream of mushroom	½ teaspoon oregano leaves, crushed	1½ pounds sharp Cheddar	French bread cubes
cream of onion	½ teaspoon marjoram leaves, crushed	1 pound natural Swiss	celery sticks
cream of celery	⅛ teaspoon hot pepper sauce	1½ pounds Gruyère	corn chips
Cheddar cheese	¼ teaspoon dry mustard	1½ pounds Monterey Jack	apple wedges

1. In 3-quart saucepan over medium heat, in hot butter, cook tomatoes, onion and garlic 10 minutes or until mixture is slightly thickened, stirring often.

2. Stir in **Soup** and **Seasoning.** Gradually add **Cheese,** stirring until smooth after each addition.

3. Pour cheese mixture into fondue pot and keep warm. Serve with **Dipper.** Makes about 3½ cups.

Tip: *If fondue becomes too thick, stir in a little milk.*

To Microwave: In 2-quart microwave-safe casserole, combine butter, tomatoes, onion and garlic; cover. Microwave on HIGH 3 to 4 minutes until onion is tender, stirring once. Stir in **Soup, Seasoning** and **Cheese.** Microwave on HIGH 4 to 6 minutes until cheese melts, stirring occasionally. Proceed as in Step 3.

Spicy Bean Spread

½ cup salad oil
Flavoring
Seasoning
1 clove garlic, minced
⅛ teaspoon pepper
1 can (16 ounces) garbanzo beans, drained
1 can (10¾ to 11½ ounces) condensed **Soup**
3 tablespoons chopped fresh parsley
Accompaniment

Flavoring	Seasoning	Soup	Accompaniment
3 tablespoons lemon juice	3 tablespoons toasted sesame seed	cream of onion	torn pita bread
¼ cup taco sauce	2 tablespoons finely chopped onion	chili beef	tortilla chips
1 tablespoon Worcestershire	2 tablespoons chopped fresh chives	split pea with ham and bacon	melba toast
2 tablespoons red wine vinegar	¼ cup chopped green chilies	bean with bacon	crackers

1. In covered blender container, blend oil, **Flavoring, Seasoning,** garlic and pepper until smooth.

2. Add beans. Cover and blend until smooth, stopping to scrape down sides as necessary.

3. In medium bowl, combine bean mixture, **Soup** and parsley; mix until smooth. Cover and chill before serving. Spread on **Accompaniment.** Makes about 3 cups.

Rumaki Spread

6 slices bacon
1 pound chicken livers
2 envelopes unflavored gelatin
Liquid
1 can (10¾ ounces) condensed **Soup**
¼ cup chopped water chestnuts
Flavoring
Accompaniment

Liquid	Soup	Flavoring	Accompaniment
¼ cup dry sherry plus ½ cup water	cream of onion	¼ cup chopped green onions	party rye rounds
¼ cup dry white wine plus ½ cup water	cream of celery	2 hard-cooked eggs, chopped	melba toast
¾ cup water	cream of mushroom	2 tablespoons chopped fresh chives	wheat crackers
¾ cup apple juice	cream of chicken	1 teaspoon curry powder	sliced French bread

1. In 10-inch skillet over medium heat, cook bacon until browned. Remove from skillet; drain on paper towels. Crumble and set aside.

2. Add chicken livers to pan drippings; cook until livers are tender, but still pink inside, stirring frequently. Remove from heat.

3. In small saucepan, sprinkle gelatin over **Liquid** to soften. Over low heat, heat until gelatin dissolves, stirring often. Remove from heat.

4. In food processor or blender container, combine **Soup,** cooked chicken livers and gelatin mixture. Process or blend until smooth. Pour into medium bowl. Stir in bacon, water chestnuts and **Flavoring.** Pour into 3-cup mold. Cover; refrigerate until set, at least 4 hours.

5. Unmold onto serving platter; serve with **Accompaniment.** Makes 16 appetizer servings.

Make-Ahead Canapés

1 can (10¾ to 11 ounces) condensed **Soup**
1 cup shredded **Cheese**
Protein
1 clove garlic, minced
2 tablespoons chopped fresh parsley
Bread
Paprika

Soup	Cheese	Protein	Bread
Cheddar cheese	sharp Cheddar	½ pound ground cooked ham	melba toast rounds
cream of celery	Swiss	4 hard-cooked eggs, chopped	party rye
cream of mushroom	Provolone	1 can (about 7 ounces) tuna, drained and flaked	thinly sliced French bread
cream of onion	Muenster	1 can (5 ounces) chunk white chicken	thinly sliced bagels

1. In medium bowl, stir together **Soup, Cheese, Protein,** garlic and parsley until well mixed. Spread mixture on **Bread** and place on baking sheets. Sprinkle with paprika. Freeze until firm. Wrap in foil or place frozen canapés in freezer bags for longer storage. Return to freezer.

2. Preheat oven to 375°F. Cut bread into smaller pieces, if necessary (for instance: cut party rye into halves, French bread into quarters). Bake frozen appetizers 15 minutes or until golden brown. Makes about 2½ cups spread, 80 appetizers.

Herbed Seafood Mousse

2 envelopes unflavored gelatin
½ cup water
Seafood
1 can (10¾ ounces) condensed **Soup**
2 eggs, separated
2 tablespoons lemon juice
2 tablespoons finely chopped onion
¼ teaspoon **Herb,** crushed
Accompaniment

Seafood	Soup	Herb	Accompaniment
1 can (15 ounces) salmon, drained	cream of celery	dill weed	rusks (see **Tip** below)
2 cans (4½ ounces each) small shrimp, drained	cream of shrimp	tarragon leaves	crackers
2 cans (about 7 ounces each) tuna, drained	cream of mushroom	basil leaves	fresh vegetables

1. In small saucepan, sprinkle gelatin over water to soften. Over low heat, heat until gelatin is dissolved, stirring constantly.

2. Place **Seafood, Soup,** egg yolks, lemon juice, onion, **Herb** and gelatin mixture in blender container or food processor. Cover; blend or process until smooth.

3. In medium bowl with mixer at high speed, beat egg whites until stiff peaks form. Fold soup mixture into whites. Pour into 6-cup mold. Cover; refrigerate until set, at least 4 hours. Unmold and serve with **Accompaniment.** Makes about 5 cups, 16 appetizer servings.

Tip: *To make rusks, cut sliced bread into quarters or cut into fancy shapes with cookie cutters. Arrange in single layer on baking sheet. Bake at 300°F. 10 to 15 minutes until bread is very dry and crisp.*

Sweet and Sour Cocktail Sausages

1 can (10¾ ounces) condensed tomato soup
¼ cup grape jelly
¼ cup vinegar
Seasoning
1 pound **Sausage**
Garnish

Seasoning	Sausage	Garnish
1 tablespoon prepared mustard	frankfurters, cut into 1-inch pieces	1 can (20 ounces) pineapple chunks, drained
1 tablespoon Worcestershire	kielbasa, cut into bite-sized pieces	2 large green peppers, cut into ¾-inch squares
few drops hot pepper sauce	smoked cocktail sausage links	10 green onions, cut into 1½-inch pieces
1 tablespoon prepared horseradish	salami, cubed	1 jar (16 ounces) dill pickles, drained and cut into ¼-inch pieces

1. In 2-quart saucepan over medium heat, heat soup, jelly, vinegar and **Seasoning** until jelly melts and mixture is very warm.

2. Meanwhile, place 1 **Sausage** chunk and 1 **Garnish** on each toothpick or cocktail pick. Add to sauce; heat through, stirring occasionally. Serve hot. Makes about 40 appetizers.

To Microwave: Place 1 **Sausage** chunk and 1 **Garnish** on each toothpick or cocktail pick. In 3-quart microwave-safe casserole, combine soup, jelly, vinegar and **Seasoning;** cover. Microwave on HIGH 3 to 5 minutes until hot, stirring once. Add sausage and garnish to casserole; cover. Microwave on HIGH 5 to 8 minutes until heated through, stirring once.

Flaky Mushroom Appetizers

2 tablespoons salad oil
1 small onion, finely chopped
2 cups chopped mushrooms
Vegetable
1 can (10¾ to 11 ounces) condensed **Soup**
Cheese
Seasoning
1 tablespoon all-purpose flour
3 eggs, beaten
¾ cup butter or margarine, melted
½ pound phyllo (strudel leaves)

Vegetable	Soup	Cheese	Seasoning
1 package (10 ounces) frozen chopped spinach, thawed and drained	cream of mushroom	½ cup grated Parmesan	½ teaspoon dill weed, crushed
1 package (10 ounces) frozen chopped broccoli, thawed and drained	creamy chicken mushroom	1 cup shredded Cheddar	½ teaspoon thyme leaves, crushed
2 cups shredded carrots	cream of onion	½ pound feta, crumbled	½ teaspoon oregano leaves, crushed
2 cups shredded zucchini	Cheddar cheese	1 cup ricotta	¼ teaspoon ground nutmeg

1. In 10-inch skillet over medium heat, in hot oil, cook onion and mushrooms until tender. Stir in **Vegetable;** cook until vegetable is tender and all liquid is evaporated. Remove from heat. Stir in **Soup, Cheese, Seasoning,** flour and eggs until well mixed.

2. Brush 15 by 10-inch jelly-roll pan with some of the melted butter. Lay 1 sheet phyllo in pan, trimming so sheet fits evenly in pan. Brush with more melted butter. (While working, cover remaining phyllo with damp towel to prevent drying.) Lay another sheet phyllo in pan, trimming edges to fit. Brush with more butter. Repeat layering, trimming and brushing phyllo with butter to use about half of the phyllo.

3. Spread mushroom mixture over phyllo in pan. Using remaining phyllo and melted butter, add layers of phyllo and butter, ending with butter.

4. Bake at 375°F. 25 minutes or until phyllo is lightly browned. Let stand 15 minutes before cutting. Makes 24 appetizers.

Tip: *If phyllo sheets are smaller than jelly-roll pan, use 2 or more sheets for each layer, overlapping slightly at seams.*

Double Cheese Puffs

1 cup water
½ cup butter or margarine
1 cup all-purpose flour
Cheese
4 eggs
1 package (8 ounces) cream cheese, softened
1 can (10¾ to 11 ounces) condensed **Soup**
1 tablespoon chopped fresh parsley
Seasoning
Flavoring
Paprika (optional)

Cheese	Soup	Seasoning	Flavoring
½ cup shredded Cheddar	cream of onion	1 teaspoon Worcestershire	2 tablespoons crumbled blue cheese
3 tablespoons grated Parmesan	Cheddar cheese	1 tablespoon lemon juice	1 teaspoon summer savory leaves, crushed
½ cup shredded Swiss	cream of celery	few drops hot pepper sauce	2 slices bacon, cooked, drained and crumbled
½ cup shredded Provolone	cream of chicken	1 tablespoon dry sherry	¼ cup chopped pimento-stuffed olives

1. Preheat oven to 375°F. Grease 2 large baking sheets.

2. To prepare puffs, in 2-quart saucepan over medium heat, heat water and butter to boiling. Remove from heat. Add flour all at once. With wooden spoon, vigorously stir until mixture forms a ball and leaves the side of pan. Stir in **Cheese.** Add eggs, one at a time, beating well after each addition until smooth.

3. Drop mixture by heaping teaspoonfuls about 1½ inches apart onto baking sheets.

4. Bake 20 to 25 minutes until lightly browned. Cool completely on wire rack.

5. For filling, in medium bowl with mixer at medium speed, beat cream cheese and **Soup** until smooth. Stir in parsley, **Seasoning** and **Flavoring.**

6. With sharp knife, remove tops from puffs. Spoon about 1 rounded teaspoonful of filling into each puff; replace top. Refrigerate until serving time, at least 1 hour. Sprinkle puffs with paprika. Makes about 50 puffs.

Miniature Quiches

4 eggs
1 can (10¾ to 11 ounces) condensed **Soup**
½ cup half-and-half
¼ teaspoon **Seasoning**
2 tablespoons grated Parmesan cheese
Pastry for 2-crust 9-inch pie
Cheese
¾ cup **Filling**
Ground nutmeg

Soup	Seasoning	Cheese	Filling
cream of celery	dill weed, crushed	1 cup shredded Swiss	chopped cooked shrimp
Cheddar cheese	oregano leaves, crushed	1 cup shredded Cheddar	diced cooked ham
cream of mushroom	curry powder	1 cup shredded American	drained, cooked chopped broccoli
cream of chicken	tarragon leaves, crushed	⅓ cup additional grated Parmesan	drained, cooked chopped asparagus

1. In medium bowl, beat together eggs, **Soup,** half-and-half, **Seasoning** and Parmesan cheese. Set aside.

2. Divide pastry in half. On floured surface, roll out one half to ⅛-inch thickness. Cut 9 rounds using 4-inch cookie cutter with scalloped edge. Line 3-inch muffin-pan cups with rounds. Repeat with remaining dough.

3. In small bowl, combine **Cheese** and **Filling.** Divide mixture equally among shells. Preheat oven to 425°F.

4. Place about 2 tablespoons of soup mixture in each prepared shell. Sprinkle with nutmeg.

5. Bake 20 to 25 minutes until set. Cool in pans on racks 5 minutes. Remove from pans and serve. Makes 18 appetizers.

Pesto Pizza Appetizers

Crust

1 can (10¾ to 11 ounces) condensed **Soup**

2 cloves garlic, minced

½ cup chopped almonds

½ teaspoon basil leaves, crushed

½ teaspoon oregano leaves, crushed

1 cup **Vegetable**

¾ cup grated Parmesan cheese

1 cup shredded **Cheese**

Crust	Soup	Vegetable	Cheese
12-inch refrigerated prepared pizza crust	Cheddar cheese	drained, cooked chopped broccoli	mozzarella
2 tubes (7½ ounces each) refrigerated biscuits	cream of chicken	frozen chopped spinach, thawed and drained	longhorn
1 pound frozen bread dough, thawed	cream of mushroom	chopped fresh parsley	sharp Cheddar

1. Preheat oven to 425°F. Grease 12-inch pizza pan. Place refrigerated crust in pizza pan; pat refrigerated biscuits into pan; or roll out thawed bread dough to fit into pan. Bake **Crust** until top is dry, about 5 minutes for prepared crust, about 10 minutes for biscuit or bread dough.

2. Meanwhile, in covered blender or food processor, combine **Soup,** garlic, almonds, basil, oregano, **Vegetable** and Parmesan cheese. Blend or process until smooth.

3. Spread soup mixture over crust. Sprinkle with **Cheese.** Bake 15 minutes more or until pizza is hot and cheese is melted. Cool slightly; cut into squares. Makes 32 appetizer servings.

Tip: *To serve this pizza as a main dish, cut into wedges.*

French Pizza Slices

½ pound bulk pork sausage
½ cup chopped onion
1 clove garlic, minced
1 can (10¾ ounces) condensed tomato soup
Vegetable
½ teaspoon **Herb,** crushed
Seasoning
1 loaf (12 to 14 inches) French bread, halved lengthwise
1 cup shredded **Cheese**

Vegetable	Herb	Seasoning	Cheese
½ cup sliced mushrooms	oregano leaves	few drops hot pepper sauce	mozzarella
½ cup chopped green pepper	basil leaves	1 teaspoon chili powder	Cheddar
½ cup sliced pitted ripe olives	marjoram leaves	2 tablespoons grated Romano cheese	American
¼ cup chopped green chilies	Italian seasoning	½ teaspoon ground cumin	Monterey Jack

1. In 10-inch skillet over medium heat, cook sausage, onion and garlic until vegetables are tender and sausage is well browned, stirring occasionally to break up meat. Pour off fat.

2. Add soup, **Vegetable, Herb** and **Seasoning.** Heat to boiling; reduce heat to low. Simmer, uncovered, 5 minutes. Remove from heat; cool slightly.

3. Arrange bread cut side up on baking sheet. Spoon soup mixture on bread; sprinkle with **Cheese.** Bake at 450°F. 15 minutes or until hot. Cut each bread half into 8 slices to serve. Makes 16 appetizers.

Tip: *To make ahead, prepare as above, but do not bake. Freeze until firm. When frozen, wrap in foil; return to freezer. Unwrap; place frozen bread on baking sheet. Bake at 450°F. 20 to 25 minutes until heated through.*

CALORIE AND SODIUM GUIDE (PER SERVING)

Recipe	Calories	Sodium (mg)
Appetizer Cheesecake (page 12)		
Row 1 (cream of celery)	270	393
Row 2 (Cheddar cheese)	292	385
Row 3 (tomato)	267	304
Row 4 (cream of chicken)	270	350
Caponata (page 14)*		
Row 1 (celery)	22	41
Row 2 (green pepper)	23	61
Row 3 (Jerusalem artichokes)	20	35
Row 4 (mushrooms)	22	38
Avocado Dip (page 15)*		
Row 1 (cream of celery)	35	105
Row 2 (cream of shrimp)	34	104
Row 3 (cream of chicken)	35	101
Mexican-Style Appetizer (page 16)		
Row 1 (olives)	154	537
Row 2 (ham)	156	346
Row 3 (avocado)	157	350
Row 4 (pepperoni)	188	561
Snappy Cocktail Dip (page 18)*		
Row 1 (cream of celery)	32	94
Row 2 (cream of mushroom)	32	93
Row 3 (cream of chicken)	28	100
Row 4 (golden mushroom)	30	105
Cheese Ball (page 19)		
Row 1 (bean with bacon)	119	355
Row 2 (chili beef)	114	347
Row 3 (split pea with ham and bacon)	241	516
Cheese-Stuffed Vegetables (page 21)		
Row 1 (cream of onion)	30	92
Row 2 (cream of celery)	30	91
Row 3 (cream of mushroom)	30	87
Tomato Cheese Fondue (page 22)*		
Row 1 (cream of mushroom)	59	124
Row 2 (cream of onion)	41	69
Row 3 (cream of celery)	60	92
Row 4 (Cheddar cheese)	59	118
Spicy Bean Spread (page 23)*		
Row 1 (lemon juice)	40	57
Row 2 (taco sauce)	39	60
Row 3 (Worcestershire)	43	58
Row 4 (red wine vinegar)	42	60

Recipe	Calories	Sodium (mg)
Rumaki Spread (page 24)		
Row 1 (dry sherry)	91	210
Row 2 (dry white wine)	124	239
Row 3 (water)	85	199
Row 4 (apple juice)	93	205
Make-Ahead Canapés (page 25)		
Row 1 (Cheddar cheese)	21	45
Row 2 (cream of celery)	23	49
Row 3 (cream of mushroom)	12	64
Row 4 (cream of onion)	10	42
Herbed Seafood Mousse (page 26)		
Row 1 (salmon)	70	278
Row 2 (shrimp)	44	200
Row 3 (tuna)	71	323
Sweet and Sour Cocktail Sausages (page 28)		
Row 1 (mustard)	58	194
Row 2 (Worcestershire)	49	207
Row 3 (hot pepper sauce)	46	165
Row 4 (horseradish)	59	326
Flaky Mushroom Appetizers (page 29)		
Row 1 (spinach)	114	249
Row 2 (broccoli)	128	257
Row 3 (carrots)	133	324
Row 4 (zucchini)	128	232
Double Cheese Puffs (page 31)		
Row 1 (Cheddar)	59	104
Row 2 (Parmesan)	56	99
Row 3 (Swiss)	59	96
Row 4 (Provolone)	60	136
Miniature Quiches (page 32)		
Row 1 (cream of celery)	172	411
Row 2 (Cheddar cheese)	185	390
Row 3 (cream of mushroom)	170	369
Row 4 (cream of chicken)	154	329
Pesto Pizza Appetizers (page 33)		
Row 1 (pizza crust)	85	228
Row 2 (biscuits)	143	270
Row 3 (bread dough)	93	225
French Pizza Slices (page 34)		
Row 1 (mushrooms)	139	404
Row 2 (green pepper)	149	424
Row 3 (olives)	155	514
Row 4 (green chilies)	147	418

*Figures are for 1 tablespoon.

Soups

Chili

1 pound **Meat**
1 cup chopped onion
1 cup chopped green pepper
2 cloves garlic, minced
2 cans (10½ to 10¾ ounces each) condensed **Soup**
1 can (about 15 ounces) **Vegetable**
2 tablespoons chili powder
1 tablespoon vinegar
Garnish

Meat	Soup	Vegetable	Garnish
ground beef	tomato rice	kidney beans	shredded Cheddar cheese
bulk pork sausage	Spanish style vegetable	mixed vegetables	green pepper rings
Italian sausage, casings removed	tomato bisque	garbanzo beans	sour cream and sliced green onions
ground pork	tomato	whole kernel corn	crushed corn chips

1. In 4-quart Dutch oven over medium heat, cook **Meat,** onion, green pepper and garlic until meat is browned and vegetables are tender, stirring occasionally to break up meat. Pour off fat.

2. Stir in **Soup, Vegetable** and its liquid, chili powder and vinegar. Heat to boiling. Reduce heat to low; simmer, uncovered, 30 minutes, stirring occasionally.

3. Ladle into bowls; top with **Garnish.** Makes about 6½ cups, 6 servings.

To Microwave: In 2-quart microwave-safe casserole, crumble **Meat.** Add onion, green pepper and garlic; cover. Microwave on HIGH 7 to 9 minutes until meat is nearly done, stirring occasionally. Pour off fat. Stir in **Soup, Vegetable** and its liquid, chili powder and vinegar; cover. Microwave on HIGH 12 to 15 minutes until heated through, stirring occasionally. Ladle into bowls; top with **Garnish.**

Split Pea and Meatball Soup

1 cup dry green split peas, rinsed and drained

1 can (10½ to 10¾ ounces) condensed **Soup**

2 cups water

1 cup chopped onion

Herb

⅛ teaspoon pepper

½ pound **Meat**

¼ cup soft bread crumbs

1 egg

1 tablespoon chopped fresh parsley

1 clove garlic, minced

1 cup chopped carrots

1 cup **Vegetable**

1 can (14½ ounces) stewed tomatoes

Soup	Herb	Meat	Vegetable
beef broth	1 teaspoon summer savory leaves, crushed	ground beef	sliced celery
French onion	1 teaspoon marjoram leaves, crushed	ground pork	frozen cut green beans
chicken broth	½ teaspoon rubbed sage	ground raw turkey	frozen mixed vegetables
Spanish style vegetable	1 teaspoon basil leaves, crushed	bulk pork sausage	diced, peeled cucumber

1. In 4-quart Dutch oven over high heat, combine peas, **Soup,** water, onion, **Herb** and pepper. Heat to boiling; reduce heat to low. Cover; simmer 1 hour.

2. Meanwhile, for meatballs, in medium bowl, combine **Meat,** bread crumbs, egg, parsley and garlic. Mix lightly, but well. Shape into 36 balls, using 1 rounded teaspoonful for each. Set aside.

3. Add carrots, **Vegetable** and tomatoes to soup mixture. Over high heat, heat to boiling. Add meatballs; reduce heat to low. Cover; simmer 30 minutes until vegetables are tender and meat is done. Makes about 8 cups, 6 servings.

Baked Sausage-Bean Soup

2 tablespoons salad oil
1 cup chopped onion
1 clove garlic, minced
1 can (10½ to 10¾ ounces) condensed **Soup**
1 can (16 to 20 ounces) **Beans**
½ cup diced **Sausage**
1 can (4 ounces) chopped green chilies, drained
1 can (16 ounces) tomatoes, cut up
½ cup water
1½ cups cubed French bread
1 cup shredded **Cheese**

Soup	Beans	Sausage	Cheese
Spanish style vegetable	white kidney beans	kielbasa	colby
minestrone	garbanzo beans	cooked chorizo	longhorn
vegetable	pork and beans in tomato sauce	frankfurters	Provolone
tomato	green beans	pepperoni	mozzarella

1. In 3-quart saucepan over medium heat, in hot oil, cook onion and garlic until tender, stirring occasionally.

2. Stir in **Soup, Beans** with their liquid, **Sausage,** chilies, tomatoes with their liquid and water. Heat to boiling. Reduce heat to low. Cover; simmer 10 minutes to blend flavors. Preheat oven to 450°F.

3. Ladle soup into six 10-ounce ovenproof bowls; place on jelly-roll pan. Sprinkle with bread and **Cheese.**

4. Bake 10 minutes until top is golden brown and cheese is melted. Makes about 6 cups, 6 servings.

Pasta and Bean Soup

Meat
½ cup chopped onion
½ cup chopped celery
½ cup shredded carrot
1 clove garlic, minced
1 can (10½ ounces) condensed **Soup**
1 soup can water
1 can (19 ounces) white kidney beans
½ teaspoon **Herb,** crushed
1 bay leaf
⅛ teaspoon pepper
½ cup uncooked **Pasta**

Meat	Soup	Herb	Pasta
½ cup diced cooked ham plus 2 tablespoons salad oil	vegetable	thyme leaves	small shell macaroni
4 slices bacon, diced	Spanish style vegetable	oregano leaves	ditalini
4 ounces bulk pork sausage, crumbled	minestrone	basil leaves	elbow macaroni

1. In 4-quart Dutch oven over medium heat, cook **Meat** until lightly browned, stirring occasionally. Add onion, celery, carrot and garlic; cook until vegetables are tender, stirring occasionally.

2. Stir in **Soup,** water, beans with their liquid, **Herb,** bay leaf and pepper. Heat to boiling. Reduce heat to low. Cover; simmer 15 minutes.

3. Stir in **Pasta;** cook about 12 minutes more or until pasta is tender. Discard bay leaf. Makes about 5 cups, 4 servings.

Hearty Bean Soup

1 cup dry **Beans**
5 cups water
¼ pound smoked pork butt or ham
1 cup chopped onion
½ cup chopped green pepper
1 clove garlic, minced
Seasoning
¼ teaspoon pepper
1 bay leaf
1 can (10¾ ounces) condensed cream of potato soup
Vegetable 1
Vegetable 2
½ cup chopped green onions

Beans	Seasoning	Vegetable 1	Vegetable 2
navy beans	½ teaspoon thyme leaves, crushed	2 cups coarsely chopped cabbage	1 cup sliced carrots
red kidney beans	2 tablespoons chili powder	2 cups diced tomatoes	1 cup whole kernel corn
garbanzo beans	1 tablespoon curry powder	1 cup cut green beans	1 small butternut squash, peeled and cubed
pinto beans	½ teaspoon ground cumin	2 cups sliced zucchini	1 cup sliced okra

1. In 4-quart Dutch oven over high heat, heat **Beans** and water to boiling. Boil, uncovered, 2 minutes. Remove from heat and let stand, covered, 1 hour.

2. Add pork, onion, green pepper, garlic, **Seasoning,** pepper and bay leaf. Over high heat, heat to boiling; reduce heat to low. Cover; simmer 1½ hours.

3. Remove pork from soup. Cool until easy to handle. Dice pork and return to soup.

4. Add potato soup, **Vegetable 1** and **Vegetable 2.** Cover; simmer 25 minutes more or until vegetables are tender. Add water, if needed, to make desired consistency. Discard bay leaf. Just before serving, stir in green onions. Makes about 5 cups, 4 servings.

Easy Pea Soup

1 cup diced potato
½ cup chopped onion
Vegetable
Herb
1 cup chicken broth
½ cup water
1 can (11¼ ounces) condensed green pea soup
½ cup **Liquid**
Garnish

Vegetable	Herb	Liquid	Garnish
1 cup carrots cut into julienne strips	½ teaspoon summer savory leaves, crushed	half-and-half	sour cream
1 cup sliced celery	1 tablespoon chopped fresh parsley	milk	crumbled cooked bacon
1 large tomato, chopped	½ teaspoon oregano leaves, crushed	additional water	fresh mint leaves
1 cup fresh or frozen peas	¼ teaspoon rubbed sage	additional chicken broth	seasoned croutons

1. In 2-quart saucepan over medium heat, heat potato, onion, **Vegetable, Herb,** chicken broth and water to boiling. Reduce heat to low. Cover; simmer 10 minutes or until vegetables are tender.

2. Meanwhile, in medium bowl, combine pea soup and **Liquid;** stir until smooth. Add to broth mixture. Heat through. Ladle into bowls; top with **Garnish.** Makes about 4 cups, 4 servings.

To Microwave: In 2-quart microwave-safe casserole, combine potato, onion, **Vegetable, Herb,** chicken broth and water; cover. Microwave on HIGH 8 to 10 minutes until vegetables are tender, stirring once. Meanwhile, in medium bowl, combine pea soup and **Liquid;** stir until smooth. Add to broth mixture; cover. Microwave on HIGH 4 to 6 minutes until heated through, stirring once. Ladle into bowls; top with **Garnish.**

Creamy Cabbage Soup

2 tablespoons butter or margarine
2 cups coarsely shredded cabbage
1 medium onion, chopped
Meat
1 can (10½ to 10¾ ounces) condensed **Soup**
Liquid
Garnish

Meat	Soup	Liquid	Garnish
4 ounces kielbasa, diced	cream of celery	½ cup light cream plus ¾ cup water	shredded Swiss cheese
4 frankfurters, sliced	cream of potato	1 soup can water	paprika
1 cup diced cooked ham	cream of chicken	1 soup can milk	pretzel sticks
4 slices bacon, cooked, drained and crumbled	cream of mushroom	½ cup evaporated milk plus ¾ cup water	croutons

1. In 3-quart saucepan over medium heat, in hot butter, cook cabbage and onion until tender, stirring occasionally. Add **Meat;** cook 2 minutes, stirring occasionally.

2. Stir in **Soup** and **Liquid** until smooth. Heat through, stirring occasionally. Ladle into bowls; sprinkle with **Garnish.** Makes about 4 cups, 4 servings.

To Microwave: In 3-quart microwave-safe casserole, combine butter, cabbage and onion; cover. Microwave on HIGH 8 to 10 minutes until cabbage and onion are tender, stirring occasionally. Add **Meat.** Stir in **Soup** and **Liquid** until smooth; cover. Microwave on HIGH 8 to 10 minutes until heated through, stirring occasionally. Ladle into bowls; sprinkle with **Garnish.**

Hearty Vegetable Soup

1 can (10¾ ounces) condensed chicken broth
1 soup can water
Vegetable
Starch
Garnish

Vegetable	Starch	Garnish
½ cup chopped tomato plus ½ cup chopped green onions	2 tablespoons raw regular rice	1 tablespoon grated Parmesan cheese
½ cup sliced carrot plus ½ cup sliced celery	¼ cup small shell macaroni	1 teaspoon chopped fresh parsley
1 cup frozen mixed vegetables	¼ cup pearled barley	1 teaspoon chopped fresh chives
½ cup sliced mushrooms plus ½ cup sliced leek	2 tablespoons raw brown rice	2 slices bacon, cooked, drained and crumbled

1. In 2-quart saucepan over high heat, heat chicken broth, water and **Vegetable** to boiling. Add **Starch.** Reduce heat to low. Cover; simmer until starch is done, about 20 minutes for regular rice or pasta, about 40 minutes for barley or brown rice.

2. Ladle soup into bowls; top with **Garnish.** Makes about 3 cups, 3 servings.

Speedy Potato Chowder

4 slices bacon, diced
½ cup chopped onion
1 can (10¾ ounces) condensed cream of potato soup
Liquid
1 can (about 8 ounces) **Vegetable**
Meat
2 tablespoons chopped fresh parsley

Liquid	Vegetable	Meat
¾ cup beer plus ¾ cup water	mixed vegetables	1 cup sliced frankfurters
1½ cups milk	whole kernel corn	1 cup diced cooked chicken
1 cup milk plus ½ cup light cream	lima beans	1 cup diced cooked ham
1 cup evaporated milk plus ½ cup water	diced carrots	1 can (about 7 ounces) tuna, drained and flaked

1. In 3-quart saucepan over medium heat, cook bacon until crisp. Remove with slotted spoon and drain on paper towels. Pour off all but 1 tablespoon bacon drippings.

2. In hot drippings, cook onion until tender, stirring occasionally. Stir in soup and **Liquid** until well mixed. Add **Vegetable** with its liquid, **Meat,** parsley and reserved bacon. Heat through, stirring occasionally. Makes about 4 cups, 4 servings.

To Microwave: In 2-quart microwave-safe casserole, place bacon; cover. Microwave on HIGH 3 to 4 minutes until crisp, stirring once. With slotted spoon, remove bacon; drain on paper towels. Pour off all but 1 tablespoon bacon drippings. To drippings, add onion; cover. Microwave on HIGH 2 to 2½ minutes until tender, stirring once. Stir in soup and **Liquid** until well mixed. Add **Vegetable** with its liquid, **Meat,** parsley and reserved bacon; cover. Microwave on HIGH 8 to 10 minutes until heated through, stirring occasionally.

Curried Vegetable Soup

2 tablespoons butter or margarine
1 cup chopped onion
1 cup sliced carrots
Vegetable
1 cup water
1 can (10¾ ounces) condensed **Soup**
½ teaspoon curry powder
1 cup shredded **Cheese**
Liquid

Vegetable	Soup	Cheese	Liquid
2 medium zucchini, diced	cream of chicken	sharp Cheddar	1 can (13 ounces) evaporated milk
2 cups fresh or frozen cut green beans	cream of asparagus	American	1½ cups light cream
2 cups fresh or frozen cut asparagus	cream of celery	Swiss	1½ cups milk
2 cups sliced celery	cream of potato	Monterey Jack	1 can (14½ ounces) chicken broth

1. In 3-quart saucepan over medium heat, in hot butter, cook onion, carrots and **Vegetable** 5 minutes, stirring occasionally. Add water; heat to boiling. Reduce heat to low. Cover; simmer 5 minutes or until vegetables are tender-crisp.

2. Stir in **Soup,** curry powder, **Cheese** and **Liquid.** Heat through. Makes about 5 cups, 6 servings.

Onion Soup au Gratin

2 tablespoons salad oil
1 tablespoon butter or margarine
1 pound onions, sliced (4 cups)
¼ teaspoon sugar
2 cans (10 to 10¾ ounces each) condensed **Soup**
2 soup cans water
Bread
2 cups shredded **Cheese**
¼ cup grated Parmesan cheese

Soup	Bread	Cheese
beef broth	6 slices French bread, toasted	Swiss
beef noodle	2 cups croutons	Gruyère
chicken broth	6 slices rye bread, toasted	Cheddar
chicken noodle	3 croissants, split horizontally and toasted	mozzarella

1. In covered 3-quart saucepan over low heat, in hot oil and butter, cook onions 15 minutes or until tender, stirring occasionally.

2. Uncover; stir in sugar. Over medium heat, cook 30 minutes more or until onions are golden, stirring frequently.

3. Add **Soup** and water. Heat to boiling; reduce heat to low. Cover; simmer 25 minutes.

4. Ladle soup into six 12-ounce ovenproof bowls; place bowls on jelly-roll pan. Place **Bread** in each bowl and top each with **Cheese** and Parmesan. Bake at 350°F. 20 minutes until cheese is melted and top is browned. Makes about 6½ cups, 6 servings.

Tip: *If you wish, stir in ½ cup dry white wine when soup is simmering.*

Soup in a Crust

1 can (10½ to 10¾ ounces) condensed **Soup**
1 soup can water
1 cup fresh or frozen **Vegetable**
½ cup chopped onion
Dash **Herb**
½ cup diced cooked **Meat**
¾ cup biscuit mix
¼ cup milk
1 tablespoon chopped fresh parsley

Soup	Vegetable	Herb	Meat
chicken broth	sliced carrots	thyme leaves, crushed	chicken
French onion	cut green beans	tarragon leaves, crushed	ham
beef broth	peas	rubbed sage	beef
chicken gumbo	whole kernel corn	marjoram leaves, crushed	pork

1. In 2-quart saucepan over high heat, heat **Soup,** water, **Vegetable,** onion and **Herb** to boiling. Reduce heat to low. Cover; simmer 15 minutes or until vegetable is tender. Stir in **Meat.** Pour into 1-quart casserole.

2. In small bowl, stir together biscuit mix, milk and parsley until well mixed. On lightly floured surface, knead dough a few strokes until smooth. Roll or pat into a circle slightly larger than casserole. Cut 1-inch hole in center. Place pastry round over casserole; press firmly to seal pastry to edge.

3. Bake at 400°F. 15 to 20 minutes until golden brown. Makes 3 servings.

Extra-Good Cream Soup

2 tablespoons butter or margarine
½ cup chopped onion
Vegetable
½ teaspoon **Herb,** crushed
1 can (10½ to 10¾ ounces) condensed **Soup**
½ cup light cream
¾ cup milk
Garnish

Vegetable	Herb	Soup	Garnish
1 medium tomato, diced	tarragon leaves	tomato	grated Parmesan cheese
1 cup sliced mushrooms	thyme leaves	cream of mushroom	chopped fresh parsley
1 cup fresh or frozen cut asparagus	dill weed	cream of asparagus	oyster crackers
1 cup sliced celery	marjoram leaves	cream of celery	melba toast

1. In 2-quart saucepan over medium heat, in hot butter, cook onion, **Vegetable** and **Herb** until vegetables are tender, stirring occasionally.

2. Stir in **Soup,** cream and milk. Heat through, stirring occasionally. Ladle into bowls; sprinkle with **Garnish.** Makes about 3½ cups, 4 servings.

To Microwave: In 2-quart microwave-safe casserole, combine butter, onion, **Vegetable** and **Herb;** cover. Microwave on HIGH 7 to 9 minutes until vegetables are tender, stirring once. Stir in **Soup,** cream and milk; cover. Microwave on HIGH 5 to 7 minutes until heated through, stirring occasionally. Ladle into bowls; sprinkle with **Garnish.**

Creamy Vegetable Bisque

2 tablespoons butter or margarine
1 cup **Vegetable**
1 cup sliced celery
½ cup chopped onion
1 can (10¾ ounces) condensed **Soup**
1 soup can milk
Seasoning
Garnish

Vegetable	Soup	Seasoning	Garnish
carrots cut into 1-inch julienne strips	cream of mushroom	⅛ teaspoon pepper	grated Romano cheese
broccoli flowerets cut into bite-sized pieces	cream of asparagus	½ teaspoon ground nutmeg	toasted slivered almonds
cauliflowerets cut into bite-sized pieces	cream of shrimp	¼ teaspoon dry mustard	chopped fresh parsley
cut asparagus	cream of celery	¼ teaspoon thyme leaves, crushed	lemon slices

1. In 2-quart saucepan over medium heat, in hot butter, cook **Vegetable,** celery and onion 5 to 10 minutes until vegetables are tender-crisp, stirring frequently.

2. Stir in **Soup,** milk and **Seasoning.** Heat through. Ladle into bowls; top with **Garnish.** Makes about 3½ cups, 4 servings.

Gazpacho

1 can (10½ ounces) condensed Spanish style vegetable soup
1 tablespoon olive oil
1 clove garlic, minced
¾ cup **Liquid**
Seasoning
Vegetable

Liquid	Seasoning	Vegetable
tomato juice	2 tablespoons lemon juice	⅓ cup chopped green pepper
V-8 vegetable juice	⅛ teaspoon pepper	2 tablespoons chopped green onion
beef broth	⅛ teaspoon hot pepper sauce	⅓ cup chopped cucumber
water	1 teaspoon Worcestershire	⅓ cup chopped tomato

1. In medium bowl, combine soup, oil, garlic, **Liquid** and **Seasoning;** stir in **Vegetable.**

2. Cover; refrigerate until serving time, at least 4 hours.
   Makes about 2½ cups, 3 servings.

Fish Stew

¼ cup salad oil
1 cup chopped onion
1 cup **Vegetable 1**
3 cloves garlic, minced
2 cans (10½ to 10¾ ounces each) condensed **Soup**
1 soup can water
1 can (6 ounces) tomato paste
Vegetable 2
1 bay leaf
Herb, crushed
2 pounds haddock or other fish fillets, cut into 1½-inch pieces
½ pound medium shrimp, shelled and deveined
12 medium clams in shells or 1 can (6½ ounces) minced clams

Vegetable 1	Soup	Vegetable 2	Herb
chopped green pepper	chicken broth	1 can (16 ounces) tomatoes, cut up (do not drain)	1 teaspoon basil leaves
chopped celery and celery leaves	chicken vegetable	2 cups diced peeled potatoes	½ teaspoon tarragon leaves
chopped zucchini	chicken gumbo	2 cups cubed eggplant	½ teaspoon oregano leaves
shredded carrot	chicken with rice	2 cups fresh or frozen whole kernel corn	1 teaspoon dill weed

1. In 5-quart Dutch oven over medium heat, in hot oil, cook onion, **Vegetable 1** and garlic until vegetables are tender, stirring occasionally.

2. Stir in **Soup,** water, tomato paste, **Vegetable 2,** bay leaf and **Herb.** Heat to boiling. Reduce heat; simmer, uncovered, 15 minutes.

3. Add fish, shrimp and clams. Cover; simmer 10 minutes or until fish flakes easily when tested with fork and clam shells are opened (discard any clams that do not open). Discard bay leaf. Makes about 10 cups, 8 servings.

Skillet Seafood Bisque

¼ cup butter or margarine

1 cup sliced mushrooms

Vegetable

1 clove garlic, minced

3 tablespoons all-purpose flour

1 can (10¾ ounces) condensed chicken broth

Seafood

Liquid

1 tablespoon chopped fresh parsley

Garnish

Vegetable	Seafood	Liquid	Garnish
2 tablespoons chopped fresh chives	1 pound medium shrimp, shelled and deveined	½ cup dry white wine plus ½ cup heavy cream	fresh dill sprigs
¼ cup chopped onion	1 pound bay scallops	1 cup half-and-half	grated Parmesan cheese
¼ cup chopped green onions	1 pound monkfish or other firm fish fillets, cubed	1 cup milk	ground nutmeg
½ cup chopped green pepper	1 pint shucked clams, drained and chopped	1 cup clam juice	cooked, crumbled bacon

1. In 10-inch skillet over medium heat, in hot butter, cook mushrooms, **Vegetable** and garlic until vegetables are tender, stirring occasionally. Stir in flour until smooth. Gradually stir in chicken broth. Heat to boiling, stirring constantly.

2. Add **Seafood.** Reduce heat to low. Cover; simmer about 5 minutes or until seafood is done. Stir in **Liquid** and parsley; heat through. Ladle into bowls; top with **Garnish.** Makes about 4½ cups, 6 servings.

Seafood Chowder

6 slices bacon, diced
1 cup chopped onion
1 can (10¾ ounces) condensed chicken broth
1 package (5½ ounces) au gratin potato mix
3½ cups milk
Vegetable
Seasoning
Seafood
Liquid

Vegetable	Seasoning	Seafood	Liquid
1 package (9 ounces) frozen cut green beans, thawed	⅛ teaspoon pepper	1 can (15 ounces) salmon, drained and broken into chunks	1 can (5⅓ ounces) evaporated milk
1 can (16 ounces) whole kernel corn, drained	⅛ teaspoon lemon-pepper seasoning	2 cans (6½ ounces each) minced clams (do not drain)	⅔ cup light cream
2 cups sliced carrots	⅛ teaspoon paprika	2 cans (about 7 ounces each) tuna, drained	⅓ cup light cream plus ⅓ cup dry white wine
2 cups fresh or frozen peas	¼ teaspoon dill weed, crushed	2 cans (4½ ounces each) shrimp, drained	½ cup sour cream

1. In 4-quart Dutch oven over medium heat, cook bacon and onion until bacon is browned and onion is tender, stirring occasionally.

2. Add chicken broth, potato mix with its sauce mix, milk, **Vegetable** and **Seasoning.** Heat to boiling. Reduce heat. Cover; simmer 15 minutes.

3. Stir in **Seafood** and **Liquid.** Cook 5 minutes or until heated through. Makes about 8 cups, 6 servings.

Oyster-Vegetable Stew

1 cup diced potato
½ cup **Vegetable**
¼ cup chopped onion
1 cup **Liquid**
1 can (10½ ounces) condensed oyster stew
Herb
Garnish

Vegetable	Liquid	Herb	Garnish
sliced carrots	chicken broth	1 tablespoon chopped fresh parsley	herbed croutons
green pepper strips	milk	1 tablespoon chopped fresh chives	melba toast
sliced zucchini	light cream	¼ teaspoon tarragon leaves, crushed	oyster crackers

1. In 2-quart saucepan over medium heat, heat potato, **Vegetable,** onion and **Liquid** to boiling. Reduce heat to low. Cover; simmer 10 minutes until vegetables are tender.

2. Stir in oyster stew and **Herb;** heat through. Ladle into bowls; top with **Garnish.** Makes about 2½ cups, 2 servings.

To Microwave: Use ingredients as above but use only ¾ cup **Liquid.** In 1½-quart microwave-safe casserole, combine potato, **Vegetable,** onion and only ¾ cup **Liquid;** cover. Microwave on HIGH 8 to 10 minutes until vegetables are tender, stirring once. Stir in oyster stew and **Herb;** cover. Microwave on HIGH 4 to 6 minutes until heated through, stirring once. Ladle into bowls; top with **Garnish.**

Oriental-Style Soup

1 egg white
½ pound **Meat**
¼ cup finely chopped water chestnuts
1 tablespoon cornstarch
1 teaspoon soy sauce
¼ teaspoon minced fresh ginger root
Vegetable 1
2 cans (10¾ ounces each) condensed chicken broth
1 soup can water
Vegetable 2
Garnish

Meat	Vegetable 1	Vegetable 2	Garnish
ground pork	1 cup sliced celery	½ cup peas	chopped green onions
raw chicken, finely chopped	1 cup carrots cut into julienne strips	½ cup sliced water chestnuts	sliced radishes
medium raw shrimp, shelled, deveined and finely chopped	1 ounce bean threads (available in Oriental markets)	½ cup snow pea pods	coriander sprigs

1. In small bowl with fork, beat egg white until foamy. Add **Meat,** water chestnuts, cornstarch, soy sauce and ginger root; mix well.

2. In 4-quart saucepan over high heat, heat 2 quarts water to boiling. Drop meat mixture by teaspoonfuls into water. Reduce heat; simmer 2 to 5 minutes until meat is done and balls rise to surface. Remove balls with slotted spoon; set aside. Discard water.

3. If using bean threads for **Vegetable 1,** cut threads into 2-inch lengths. In bowl, add enough hot water to bean threads to cover; let stand 15 minutes. Drain. (If using other variations, proceed to Step 4.)

4. In same saucepan over high heat, heat chicken broth and 1 soup can water to boiling. Add **Vegetable 1;** reduce heat. Simmer 5 minutes. Add **Vegetable 2;** simmer 2 minutes more.

5. Add balls to broth; heat through. Ladle into bowls; top with **Garnish.** Makes about 6 cups, 6 servings.

Tip: *Chop chicken or shrimp in food processor for best results.*

Soup Mates

One easy way to create a new soup is to combine two different condensed soups. Over the years, we have experimented with hundreds of combinations; here are some of our favorites.

To prepare soup mates, simply empty the soups into a saucepan. Gradually stir in the liquid; heat to simmer, stirring occasionally.

Soup 1		Soup 2		Liquid
split pea with ham & bacon	+	cream of celery	+	1 can milk plus 1 can water
golden mushroom	+	French onion	+	1 can milk plus 1 can water
tomato	+	green pea	+	1 can milk plus 1 can water
Cheddar cheese	+	cream of asparagus	+	1 can milk plus 1 can water
chicken noodle	+	chicken & stars	+	2 cans water
New England clam chowder	+	cream of mushroom	+	1 can milk plus 1 can water
bean with bacon	+	tomato rice	+	2 cans water
chicken gumbo	+	cream of celery	+	1 can milk plus 1 can water
Cheddar cheese	+	tomato	+	1 can milk plus 1 can water
chili beef	+	vegetable beef	+	2 cans water
cream of chicken	+	green pea	+	1 can milk plus 1 can water
black bean	+	golden mushroom	+	2 cans water
tomato	+	beef noodle	+	2 cans water
cream of celery	+	vegetarian vegetable	+	1 can milk plus 1 can water
oyster stew	+	cream of potato	+	2 cans milk
cream of mushroom	+	beef broth	+	2 cans water
minestrone	+	Manhattan clam chowder	+	2 cans water
turkey noodle	+	cream of celery	+	1 can milk plus 1 can water
meatball alphabet	+	Cheddar cheese	+	1 can milk plus 1 can water
cream of mushroom	+	tomato	+	1 can milk plus 1 can water
bean with bacon	+	French onion	+	2 cans water
chicken vegetable	+	cream of chicken	+	1 can milk plus 1 can water
New England clam chowder	+	cream of asparagus	+	2 cans milk
chicken gumbo	+	vegetable	+	2 cans water

CALORIE AND SODIUM GUIDE (PER SERVING)

Recipe	Calories	Sodium (mg)
Chili (page 36)		
Row 1 (ground beef)	325	834
Row 2 (bulk pork sausage)	387	1700
Row 3 (Italian sausage)	493	1405
Row 4 (ground pork)	447	954
Split Pea and Meatball Soup (page 38)		
Row 1 (beef broth)	163	441
Row 2 (French onion)	253	588
Row 3 (chicken broth)	134	524
Row 4 (Spanish style vegetable)	182	548
Baked Sausage-Bean Soup (page 39)		
Row 1 (Spanish style vegetable)	544	742
Row 2 (minestrone)	582	923
Row 3 (vegetable)	368	1395
Row 4 (tomato)	294	1156
Pasta and Bean Soup (page 41)		
Row 1 (ham)	490	604
Row 2 (bacon)	414	543
Row 3 (bulk pork sausage)	438	877
Hearty Bean Soup (page 42)		
Row 1 (navy beans)	260	943
Row 2 (red kidney beans)	303	881
Row 3 (garbanzo beans)	284	859
Row 4 (pinto beans)	381	840
Easy Pea Soup (page 43)		
Row 1 (carrots)	208	999
Row 2 (celery)	180	1027
Row 3 (tomato)	163	975
Row 4 (peas)	189	1071
Creamy Cabbage Soup (page 44)		
Row 1 (kielbasa)	283	1022
Row 2 (frankfurters)	289	1374
Row 3 (ham)	264	1061
Row 4 (bacon)	230	794
Hearty Vegetable Soup (page 45)		
Row 1 (tomato plus green onion)	64	837
Row 2 (carrot plus celery)	115	894
Row 3 (mixed vegetables)	146	836
Row 4 (mushrooms plus leek)	97	925

Recipe	Calories	Sodium (mg)
Speedy Potato Chowder (page 46)		
Row 1 (beer plus water)	237	1087
Row 2 (milk)	253	922
Row 3 (milk plus cream)	306	918
Row 4 (evaporated milk plus water)	278	1238
Curried Vegetable Soup (page 48)		
Row 1 (zucchini)	293	657
Row 2 (green beans)	294	790
Row 3 (asparagus)	222	562
Row 4 (celery)	166	656
Onion Soup au Gratin (page 49)		
Row 1 (beef broth)	311	1035
Row 2 (beef noodle)	356	1180
Row 3 (chicken broth)	374	1236
Row 4 (chicken noodle)	331	1064
Soup in a Crust (page 50)		
Row 1 (chicken broth)	222	1199
Row 2 (French onion)	256	1523
Row 3 (beef broth)	253	1155
Row 4 (chicken gumbo)	327	1276
Extra-Good Cream Soup (page 51)		
Row 1 (tomato)	214	631
Row 2 (mushrooms)	224	712
Row 3 (asparagus)	220	781
Row 4 (celery)	223	781
Creamy Vegetable Bisque (page 52)		
Row 1 (carrots)	199	868
Row 2 (broccoli)	190	829
Row 3 (cauliflower)	189	812
Row 4 (asparagus)	196	788
Gazpacho (page 54)		
Row 1 (tomato juice)	104	916
Row 2 (V-8 vegetable juice)	113	1133
Row 3 (beef broth)	91	1195
Row 4 (water)	89	595
Fish Stew (page 55)		
Row 1 (green pepper)	297	703
Row 2 (celery)	348	662
Row 3 (zucchini)	327	661
Row 4 (carrot)	330	688

CALORIE AND SODIUM GUIDE (PER SERVING)

Recipe	Calories	Sodium (mg)
Skillet Seafood Bisque (page 57)		
Row 1 (chives)	250	626
Row 2 (onion)	239	698
Row 3 (green onions)	254	620
Row 4 (green pepper)	168	885
Seafood Chowder (page 58)		
Row 1 (green beans)	385	1304
Row 2 (corn)	579	1887
Row 3 (carrots)	407	1556
Row 4 (peas)	440	1121

Recipe	Calories	Sodium (mg)
Oyster-Vegetable Stew (page 59)		
Row 1 (carrots)	151	1692
Row 2 (green pepper)	191	1334
Row 3 (zucchini)	351	1320
Oriental-Style Soup (page 60)		
Row 1 (ground pork)	193	919
Row 2 (chicken)	123	913
Row 3 (shrimp)	91	940

Main Dishes

✣

Fruited Chops

2 tablespoons salad oil
1½ pounds **Chops,** each cut ½ inch thick
1 can (10¾ ounces) condensed chicken broth
2 tablespoons soy sauce
1 tablespoon vinegar
Fruit
2 tablespoons brown sugar
2 tablespoons cornstarch
1 teaspoon ground **Spice**
Hot cooked rice
Garnish

Chops	Fruit	Spice	Garnish
pork	1 large apple, cubed, plus ½ cup apple juice	ginger	sliced green onion
lamb	4 orange slices, cut up, plus ½ cup orange juice	nutmeg	slivered orange peel
smoked pork	1 can (8 ounces) pineapple slices, cut up	mace	chopped fresh parsley
veal	1 can (8 ounces) apricot halves, cut up	cinnamon	sliced water chestnuts

1. In 10-inch skillet over medium-high heat, in hot oil, cook **Chops** until browned on both sides.

2. Stir in chicken broth, soy sauce and vinegar. Heat to boiling; reduce heat to low. Cover; simmer 20 minutes or until chops are tender.

3. Meanwhile, drain **Fruit,** reserving liquid. Add enough water to liquid to make ½ cup, if necessary. In small bowl, combine liquid, brown sugar, cornstarch and **Spice;** stir until smooth.

4. Remove chops from skillet; keep warm. Stir cornstarch mixture into skillet. Over medium heat, heat to boiling. Add reserved fruit; heat through.

5. Arrange chops over rice; spoon sauce over chops. Top with **Garnish.** Makes 4 servings.

Oriental Skillet

1 pound **Cutlets**
¼ cup butter or margarine
½ cup sliced green onions
2 cloves garlic, minced
1 can (10¾ ounces) condensed chicken broth
Seasoning
Vegetable
½ cup sliced water chestnuts
1 to 2 tablespoons cornstarch
3 tablespoons water
Garnish

Cutlets	Seasoning	Vegetable	Garnish
turkey	½ teaspoon lemon-pepper seasoning	1 large cucumber, halved, seeded and cut into ½-inch chunks	1 tablespoon chopped pimento
chicken	¼ teaspoon ground ginger	1 cup fresh or frozen snow pea pods	2 tablespoons sliced pitted ripe olives
veal	¼ teaspoon Chinese five-spice powder	1 cup sliced zucchini	¼ cup shredded carrot

1. With meat mallet, pound **Cutlets** to ¼-inch thickness, if necessary. In 10-inch skillet over medium heat, in hot butter, cook cutlets until browned on both sides. Remove from skillet.

2. Add green onions and garlic to skillet; cook 2 minutes, stirring constantly. Add broth and **Seasoning;** heat to boiling. Add cutlets. Reduce heat to low. Cover; simmer 15 minutes or until cutlets are nearly tender, stirring occasionally.

3. Stir in **Vegetable** and water chestnuts; simmer 5 minutes or until vegetable is tender.

4. Remove cutlets and vegetables to platter; keep warm. In cup, stir together cornstarch and water. Stir into juices in skillet. Over medium heat, heat to boiling, stirring constantly. Cook 1 minute more. Pour over cutlets and vegetables; top with **Garnish**. Makes 4 servings.

Meat-Vegetable Packets

1 can (10¾ to 11 ounces) condensed **Soup**
1 cup **Vegetable**
½ teaspoon **Herb,** crushed
4 medium carrots, thinly sliced
4 medium potatoes, thinly sliced
1 medium onion, sliced
¼ teaspoon pepper
Meat

Soup	Vegetable	Herb	Meat
golden mushroom	fresh or frozen peas	thyme leaves	4 pork chops, each cut ½ inch thick
cream of chicken	sliced mushrooms	rosemary leaves	2 pounds chicken parts
Cheddar cheese	fresh or frozen cut green beans	dill weed	4 ground beef patties (¼ pound each)
cream of celery	sliced zucchini	marjoram leaves	4 veal chops, each cut ½ inch thick

1. Tear off four 12-inch lengths of heavy foil.

2. In medium bowl, stir together **Soup, Vegetable, Herb,** carrots, potatoes, onion and pepper. Divide mixture onto foil; top each with ¼ of the **Meat.** Fold foil around food to make a tight package.

3. Bake at 350°F. 1¼ hours or until meat and vegetables are tender. Makes 4 servings.

Tip: *Packets can be cooked on charcoal or gas grill over medium coals.*

Teriyaki Beef Kabobs

1 can (10½ to 11 ounces) condensed **Soup**
¼ cup dry sherry
¼ cup soy sauce
1 large clove garlic, minced
Seasoning
1 tablespoon **Sweetener**
1½ pounds boneless beef sirloin steak, cut 1 inch thick
1 medium green pepper, cut into 1-inch squares
1 pound small whole onions, cooked and drained
½ cup pineapple chunks
Accompaniment

Soup	Seasoning	Sweetener	Accompaniment
Spanish style vegetable	¼ cup sliced green onions	honey	hot cooked rice
French onion	¼ cup finely chopped onion	brown sugar	hot cooked wild rice
beef broth	½ teaspoon ground ginger	sugar	hot cooked bulgur wheat
tomato bisque	1 teaspoon dry mustard	molasses	hot cooked noodles

1. For marinade, in medium bowl, combine **Soup,** sherry, soy sauce, garlic, **Seasoning** and **Sweetener.**

2. Cut beef into 1-inch cubes; add to marinade. Cover; refrigerate 3 hours or overnight, turning once or twice.

3. Drain meat, reserving marinade. Thread beef cubes, green pepper, onions and pineapple chunks on six 12-inch skewers.

4. On rack in broiler pan, broil 6 inches from heat 10 minutes or until meat is cooked to desired doneness, turning and brushing often with marinade. Serve with **Accompaniment.** Makes 6 servings.

Tip: *Assemble skewers before marinating. Place in shallow dish; pour marinade over skewers. Cover; refrigerate 3 hours or overnight, turning occasionally.*

Vegetable-Stuffed Beef Bundles

Vegetable
2 medium carrots, cut into 3 by ½-inch strips
6 beef cubed steaks (about 6 by 4 inches each)
2 tablespoons salad oil
1 can (10¾ ounces) condensed **Soup**
¼ cup **Liquid**
¼ teaspoon **Herb,** crushed
1 cup sour cream

Vegetable	Soup	Liquid	Herb
24 whole green beans (about ¼ pound)	cream of onion	water	thyme leaves
1 medium zucchini, cut into 3 by ½-inch sticks	creamy chicken mushroom	dry white wine	summer savory leaves
6 dill pickle spears	cream of mushroom	milk	dill weed

1. Arrange ⅙ of the **Vegetable** and carrots on each cubed steak; roll up and secure with toothpicks or string.

2. In 10-inch skillet over medium heat, in hot oil, cook beef rolls until browned on all sides. Remove from skillet.

3. Add **Soup, Liquid** and **Herb** to skillet, stirring until blended. Add beef rolls; heat to boiling. Reduce heat to low. Cover; simmer 30 minutes or until meat and vegetables are tender. Remove rolls to platter; keep warm. Stir sour cream into skillet; heat through but do not boil.

4. Spoon some sauce over rolls; pass remaining sauce. Makes 6 servings.

Beef Stew

2 pounds beef for stew, cut into 1-inch cubes
¼ cup all-purpose flour
4 tablespoons **Fat**
2 medium onions, sliced
2 cloves garlic, minced
1 teaspoon **Herb,** crushed
1 bay leaf
1 can (10½ to 11 ounces) condensed **Soup**
½ cup water
Vegetable
2 medium carrots, cut into 2 by ½-inch strips
1 cup fresh or frozen cut green beans

Fat	Herb	Soup	Vegetable
salad oil	marjoram leaves	beef broth	1 medium turnip, peeled and cubed
shortening	thyme leaves	beefy mushroom	3 medium potatoes, peeled and cubed
butter or margarine	rosemary leaves	French onion	3 medium parsnips, peeled and cut into 1-inch chunks
bacon drippings	basil leaves	beef broth with barley	3 medium sweet potatoes, peeled and cubed

1. Coat beef cubes with flour; reserve leftover flour.

2. In 4-quart Dutch oven over medium-high heat, in 2 tablespoons hot **Fat,** cook beef, a few pieces at a time, until browned on all sides. Remove beef as it browns. Reduce heat to medium.

3. Add remaining 2 tablespoons **Fat** to skillet. In hot fat, cook onions, garlic, **Herb** and bay leaf until onions are tender, stirring occasionally. Stir in reserved flour. Gradually add **Soup** and water; heat to boiling. Return meat to pan. Reduce heat to low. Cover; simmer 1 hour, stirring occasionally.

4. Add **Vegetable,** carrots and green beans. Cover; simmer 25 minutes or until vegetables are tender. Discard bay leaf. Makes about 6 cups, 8 servings.

Garden Swiss Steak

¼ cup all-purpose flour
1 pound round steak, cut ½ inch thick
2 tablespoons salad oil
1 clove garlic, minced
1 bay leaf
⅛ teaspoon pepper
1 can (10¾ ounces) condensed **Soup**
½ cup water
1 medium green pepper, cut into strips
Vegetable 1
½ cup **Vegetable 2**
Accompaniment

Soup	Vegetable 1	Vegetable 2	Accompaniment
tomato	1 medium onion, sliced	sliced mushrooms	hot mashed potatoes
cream of onion	1 cup sliced zucchini	sliced carrots	hot buttered noodles
cream of mushroom	6 green onions, sliced	chopped tomatoes	hot cooked rice
cream of potato	1 cup sliced celery	sliced parsnips	hot biscuits

1. On cutting board with meat mallet, pound flour into both sides of steak until all flour is absorbed and meat is slightly flattened. Cut steak into 4 serving-size pieces. In 10-inch skillet over medium-high heat, in hot oil, cook steak until browned on both sides.

2. Add garlic, bay leaf and pepper. Spoon **Soup** over meat; add water. Heat to boiling. Reduce heat to low. Cover; simmer 1 hour, stirring occasionally.

3. Add green pepper, **Vegetable 1** and **Vegetable 2.** Cover; simmer 30 minutes more or until meat is tender. Discard bay leaf. Serve with **Accompaniment.** Makes 4 servings.

Easy Pot Roast

Fat
3½-pound beef chuck pot roast
1 can (10¾ ounces) condensed **Soup**
Herb
2 tablespoons all-purpose flour
¼ cup **Liquid**

Fat	Soup	Herb	Liquid
2 tablespoons shortening	cream of onion	1 teaspoon thyme leaves, crushed	water
2 tablespoons salad oil	cream of mushroom	1 teaspoon rosemary leaves, crushed	dry white wine
non-stick cooking spray	cream of celery	1 teaspoon marjoram leaves, crushed	heavy cream
2 tablespoons bacon drippings	golden mushroom	1 bay leaf (remove before serving)	dry red wine

1. In 6-quart Dutch oven over medium-high heat, in hot **Fat,** brown beef on all sides. Pour off fat.

2. Stir in **Soup** and **Herb.** Reduce heat to low. Cover; simmer 2½ to 3 hours until tender, stirring occasionally. Add water during cooking, if necessary.

3. Remove beef to platter; keep warm. In screw-top jar, shake together flour and **Liquid** until smooth; stir into pan drippings. Over high heat, heat to boiling, stirring constantly. Cook 1 minute more.

4. Cut meat into thin slices. Serve gravy with meat. Makes 8 servings.

Stir-Fried Beef and Vegetables

½ pound boneless beef sirloin steak
1 can (10½ to 10¾ ounces) condensed **Soup**
1 tablespoon cornstarch
1 tablespoon soy sauce
3 tablespoons salad oil
1 clove garlic, minced
4 green onions, cut into 1-inch pieces
1 cup **Vegetable 1**
Vegetable 2
Accompaniment

Soup	Vegetable 1	Vegetable 2	Accompaniment
beef broth	fresh or frozen cut broccoli	1 can (8 ounces) sliced bamboo shoots, drained	shredded lettuce
French onion	sliced mushrooms	1 cup diced tomatoes	hot cooked rice
chicken broth	fresh or frozen cut asparagus	1 can (8 ounces) sliced water chestnuts, drained	hot cooked noodles
chicken with rice	sliced celery	1 cup fresh or canned bean sprouts	chow mein noodles

1. Freeze steak 1 hour to make slicing easier. Trim and discard excess fat from steak. Cut steak into very thin slices; set aside.

2. In small bowl, combine **Soup,** cornstarch and soy sauce; stir to blend. Set aside.

3. In 10-inch skillet or wok over medium-high heat, in 2 tablespoons hot oil, stir-fry beef strips and garlic until meat is browned; remove from skillet.

4. Add remaining 1 tablespoon oil to skillet. Add green onions and **Vegetable 1;** stir-fry 1 minute. Add **Vegetable 2;** stir-fry 30 seconds more.

5. Return beef to skillet. Stir soup mixture; stir into skillet. Heat to boiling; cook 1 minute more. Spoon over **Accompaniment.** Makes about 2½ cups, 2 servings.

Tip: *To make delicious sandwiches, spoon beef mixture into pita bread halves; omit* **Accompaniment.**

Ribs and Lentils

1 tablespoon salad oil
2 pounds **Meat**
1 can (10½ ounces) condensed French onion soup
1 cup sliced celery and leaves
2 cloves garlic, minced
¼ teaspoon pepper
½ teaspoon **Herb,** crushed
1 pound dry lentils, rinsed
1 can (10½ to 11 ounces) condensed **Soup**
1 cup sliced carrots
4 cups water
Garnish

Meat	Herb	Soup	Garnish
lamb breast, cut into 2-rib pieces	thyme leaves	Spanish style vegetable	sliced green onion
beef short ribs, cut into 1-rib pieces	marjoram leaves	tomato bisque	chopped fresh parsley
pork spareribs, cut into 2-rib pieces	basil leaves	tomato rice	chopped tomatoes

1. In 6-quart Dutch oven over medium-high heat, in hot oil, cook **Meat** until browned on all sides. Pour off fat.

2. Add French onion soup, celery, garlic, pepper and **Herb.** Heat to boiling; reduce heat to low. Cover; simmer 1 hour.

3. Add lentils, **Soup,** carrots and water. Cover; simmer 1 hour or until meat and lentils are tender. Sprinkle with **Garnish** before serving. Makes about 11 cups, 8 servings.

Brown Rice Supper

2 tablespoons salad oil
Meat
½ cup **Vegetable**
1 medium onion, sliced
1 clove garlic, minced
1 cup raw brown rice
1 can (10½ to 10¾ ounces) condensed **Soup**
1 can (14½ ounces) stewed tomatoes
½ cup water
1 teaspoon **Herb,** crushed

Meat	Vegetable	Soup	Herb
2 pounds chicken thighs and drumsticks	chopped green pepper	chicken broth	basil leaves
4 pork chops, each cut ½ inch thick	sliced mushrooms	beef broth	thyme leaves
4 smoked pork chops, each cut ½ inch thick	chopped celery	chicken gumbo	marjoram leaves
1 pound shrimp, peeled and deveined	sliced zucchini	chicken with rice	tarragon leaves

1. In 6-quart Dutch oven over medium heat, in hot oil, cook chicken or pork until browned on all sides. (Do not cook shrimp.) Remove from pan.

2. To drippings, add **Vegetable,** onion and garlic; cook until vegetables are tender, stirring frequently. Add rice; cook 1 minute, stirring constantly. Stir in **Soup,** tomatoes with their liquid, water and **Herb.**

3. Arrange chicken or pork over rice (do not add shrimp). Heat to boiling. Reduce heat to low. Cover; simmer 1 hour or until rice is tender, stirring occasionally. Add more water during cooking, if mixture appears dry. (If using shrimp, add for last 10 minutes cooking time.) Uncover; let stand 5 minutes before serving. Makes 4 servings.

Baked Chicken Florida

1 can (10½ to 10¾ ounces) condensed **Soup**
Juice
Seasoning
¼ teaspoon tarragon leaves, crushed
3 pounds chicken parts
1 tablespoon cornstarch
Garnish

Soup	Juice	Seasoning	Garnish
Spanish style vegetable	½ cup orange juice	½ teaspoon minced fresh ginger root	orange wedges
chicken broth	¼ cup lemon juice plus ¼ cup water	1 clove garlic, minced	avocado slices
chicken with rice	¼ cup lime juice plus ¼ cup water	2 tablespoons chopped fresh chives	kiwi fruit slices

1. For marinade, in small bowl, combine **Soup, Juice, Seasoning** and tarragon. In shallow baking dish, pour marinade over chicken. Cover; refrigerate at least 2 hours, turning chicken occasionally. Drain chicken, reserving marinade.

2. In shallow roasting pan, arrange chicken. Bake at 375°F. 50 minutes or until chicken is fork-tender, basting chicken frequently with marinade. Remove to serving platter; keep warm.

3. Pour remaining marinade and pan drippings into 1-quart saucepan; stir in cornstarch. Over medium heat, heat to boiling, stirring occasionally; cook 1 minute more. Spoon some sauce over chicken; pass remainder. Arrange **Garnish** around chicken. Makes 6 servings.

Chicken Breasts in Mushroom Sauce

3 whole chicken breasts, skinned, boned and split
⅓ cup all-purpose flour
2 tablespoons salad oil
2 tablespoons butter or margarine
1 clove garlic, halved
1 cup sliced mushrooms
Vegetable
1 can (10½ to 10¾ ounces) condensed **Soup**
¼ cup **Wine**
Dash pepper
Accompaniment

Vegetable	Soup	Wine	Accompaniment
¼ cup sliced green onions	chicken gumbo	dry vermouth	hot cooked rice
½ cup sliced celery	chicken with rice	dry sherry	hot mashed potatoes
½ cup shredded carrot	chicken broth	dry white wine	hot cooked noodles
¼ cup sliced leek	chicken vegetable	dry red wine	hot cooked bulgur wheat

1. With meat mallet, pound chicken to ¼-inch thickness. Coat with flour.

2. In 10-inch skillet over medium heat, in hot oil and butter, cook garlic 30 seconds; discard garlic.

3. Cook chicken cutlets, 2 or 3 at a time, until lightly browned on both sides; remove from skillet. Repeat with remaining cutlets.

4. Add mushrooms and **Vegetable** to skillet; cook until vegetables are tender, stirring occasionally. Stir in **Soup, Wine** and pepper, scraping bottom to loosen brown bits. Return cutlets to skillet. Reduce heat to low. Cover; simmer 15 minutes or until chicken is fork-tender. Serve cutlets with sauce and **Accompaniment.** Makes 6 servings.

Crispy Baked Chicken

1 can (10¾ to 11 ounces) condensed **Soup**
Seasoning
½ cup water
Crumbs
¼ cup **Addition**
⅓ cup all-purpose flour
2 pounds chicken parts

Soup	Seasoning	Crumbs	Addition
Cheddar cheese	½ teaspoon oregano leaves, crushed	2 cups finely crushed corn flakes	sesame seed
cream of mushroom	¼ teaspoon rubbed sage	1½ cups seasoned fine dry bread crumbs	finely chopped walnuts
cream of chicken	½ teaspoon basil leaves, crushed	2 cups finely crushed potato chips	wheat germ
creamy chicken mushroom	1 teaspoon chili powder	2 cups finely crushed corn chips	finely chopped almonds

1. In deep pie plate, stir together **Soup, Seasoning** and water until smooth. On waxed paper, combine **Crumbs** and **Addition.** On second sheet of waxed paper, place flour. Coat chicken with flour, then soup mixture, then crumb mixture. Place on wire rack in jelly-roll pan.

2. Bake at 375°F. 50 minutes or until chicken is fork-tender. Makes 4 servings.

Tip: *Chicken may be skinned before coating, if desired.*

Chicken Paprika

2 tablespoons salad oil
2 pounds chicken parts
1 can (10¾ ounces) condensed **Soup**
Vegetable
1 medium onion, sliced and separated into rings
1 clove garlic, minced
2 teaspoons paprika
½ cup sour cream
Accompaniment

Soup	Vegetable	Accompaniment
cream of chicken	1 cup quartered mushrooms	hot cooked noodles
cream of onion	½ cup diced celery	hot cooked rice
cream of mushroom	1 cup chopped tomatoes	hot cooked wild rice
cream of celery	½ cup diced carrots	hot cooked kasha

1. In 10-inch skillet over medium heat, in hot oil, cook chicken until browned on all sides. Pour off fat. Stir in **Soup, Vegetable,** onion, garlic and paprika. Heat to boiling. Reduce heat to low. Cover; simmer 30 to 40 minutes until chicken is fork-tender.

2. Remove chicken to platter; keep warm. Stir sour cream into sauce; over low heat, heat through, stirring constantly. Spoon some of sauce over chicken. Serve chicken with **Accompaniment;** pass remaining sauce. Makes 4 servings.

Lemon-Herbed Chicken

2 tablespoons salad oil
2 pounds chicken parts
1 can (10¾ ounces) condensed **Soup**
2 tablespoons lemon juice
½ teaspoon paprika
Seasoning
¼ teaspoon **Herb**
1 lemon, sliced
Accompaniment

Soup	Seasoning	Herb	Accompaniment
cream of chicken	⅛ teaspoon pepper	tarragon leaves, crushed	hot cooked rice
cream of celery	¼ teaspoon lemon-pepper seasoning	marjoram leaves, crushed	hot cooked noodles
cream of mushroom	¼ teaspoon dry mustard	rosemary leaves, crushed	hot mashed potatoes
creamy chicken mushroom	⅛ teaspoon cayenne pepper	rubbed sage	hot stuffing

1. In 10-inch skillet over medium heat, in hot oil, cook chicken until browned on all sides. Pour off fat.

2. Stir in **Soup,** lemon juice, paprika, **Seasoning** and **Herb.** Heat to boiling; reduce heat to low. Cover; simmer 30 to 40 minutes or until chicken is tender, stirring occasionally. Garnish chicken with lemon slices. Serve with **Accompaniment.** Makes 4 servings.

To Microwave: Use ingredients as above but omit oil. In 12 by 8-inch microwave-safe dish, arrange chicken with thicker pieces toward edge of dish; cover. Microwave on HIGH 8 to 10 minutes, rotating dish once. Pour off fat and rearrange pieces. In small bowl, combine **Soup,** lemon juice, paprika, **Seasoning** and **Herb.** Spoon evenly over chicken; cover. Microwave on HIGH 8 to 10 minutes until chicken is fork-tender, rotating dish once. Let stand, covered, 2 to 5 minutes. Remove chicken to serving platter. Stir soup mixture until smooth and creamy. Pour over chicken. Top with lemon slices; serve with **Accompaniment.**

Cornish Hens and Vegetables

2 tablespoons salad oil
2 tablespoons butter or margarine
2 Cornish hens (about 1½ pounds each), split lengthwise
1 cup **Vegetable 1**
Vegetable 2
2 cloves garlic, minced
½ teaspoon **Herb**
1 can (10½ to 11 ounces) condensed **Soup**
1 tablespoon cornstarch
2 tablespoons cold water

Vegetable 1	Vegetable 2	Herb	Soup
sliced mushrooms	4 green onions, sliced	tarragon leaves, crushed	chicken broth
sliced zucchini	2 tablespoons chopped pimento	thyme leaves, crushed	French onion
chopped tomato	½ cup chopped onion	basil leaves, crushed	tomato bisque
sliced celery	½ cup diced carrot	rubbed sage	Spanish style vegetable

1. In 10-inch skillet over medium-high heat, in hot oil and butter, cook hens until browned on both sides, 2 halves at a time. Remove to 12 by 8-inch baking dish. Reserve drippings in skillet.

2. Reduce heat to medium. Add **Vegetable 1, Vegetable 2,** garlic and **Herb.** Cook 2 minutes, stirring constantly. Add **Soup;** heat to boiling. Pour hot mixture over hens. Cover with foil.

3. Bake at 350°F. 25 minutes. Uncover; baste hens with pan juices. Bake, uncovered, 10 minutes more or until hens are fork-tender.

4. Remove hens to warm platter and keep warm. Pour pan juices into skillet; over high heat, heat to boiling. In cup, stir together cornstarch and water; stir into boiling liquid. Boil 1 minute. Spoon some sauce over hens; pass remaining sauce. Makes 4 servings.

Sautéed Chicken Livers

¼ cup butter or margarine
1 pound chicken livers
Flavoring
2 tablespoons all-purpose flour
1 can (10½ to 10¾ ounces) condensed **Soup**
½ cup water
Dash pepper
Accompaniment

Flavoring	Soup	Accompaniment
1 medium onion, coarsely chopped	chicken broth	toast
1 cup sliced mushrooms	French onion	baked potatoes, split
1 cup chopped apple	chicken gumbo	hot cooked rice
1 large green pepper, cut into strips	Spanish style vegetable	hot cooked noodles

1. In 10-inch skillet over medium-high heat, in hot butter, cook livers and **Flavoring** 8 to 10 minutes until livers are done, stirring frequently.

2. With slotted spoon, remove livers and flavoring from skillet. Into pan drippings, stir flour. Gradually add **Soup,** water and pepper, stirring constantly. Over medium heat, heat to boiling, stirring occasionally. Cook 1 minute more.

3. Add liver mixture; heat through. Serve over **Accompaniment.** Makes about 3 cups, 4 servings.

Meatball Stew

1 pound ground beef
Crumbs
½ teaspoon **Herb,** crushed
1 egg
1 clove garlic, minced
2 tablespoons salad oil
1 can (10½ to 11 ounces) condensed **Soup**
¼ cup water
3 medium potatoes, peeled and quartered
Vegetable
1 medium onion, cut into thin wedges
1 tablespoon chopped fresh parsley

Crumbs	Herb	Soup	Vegetable
½ cup soft bread crumbs	summer savory leaves	French onion	3 medium carrots, cut into 1-inch chunks
¼ cup seasoned fine dry bread crumbs	basil leaves	tomato bisque	1½ cups celery cut into ½-inch chunks
¼ cup finely crushed saltines	oregano leaves	vegetable beef	1½ cups cut green beans
¼ cup quick-cooking oats	thyme leaves	Spanish style vegetable	3 medium parsnips, peeled and cut into 1-inch chunks

1. In medium bowl, combine ground beef, **Crumbs, Herb,** egg and garlic; mix thoroughly. Shape into 20 meatballs.

2. In 10-inch skillet over medium heat, in hot oil, cook meatballs until browned on all sides. Pour off fat.

3. Stir **Soup** and water into skillet; stir in potatoes, **Vegetable** and onion. Heat to boiling. Reduce heat to low. Cover; simmer 30 minutes or until vegetables are tender, adding more water if needed. Garnish with parsley. Makes 4 servings.

Tip: *Don't overmix meat mixture or meat will become tough.*

Savory Meatballs

1 can (10¾ ounces) condensed **Soup**
½ cup water
2 tablespoons chopped fresh parsley
1 pound ground beef
Crumbs
¼ cup **Vegetable**
1 egg, beaten
½ teaspoon **Herb,** crushed
1 tablespoon salad oil

Soup	Crumbs	Vegetable	Herb
cream of onion	¼ cup fine dry bread crumbs	finely chopped onion	thyme leaves
cream of mushroom	¼ cup finely crushed saltines	shredded carrot	marjoram leaves
cream of celery	½ cup soft bread crumbs	finely chopped green pepper	basil leaves
golden mushroom	¼ cup finely crushed corn flakes	finely chopped celery	dill weed

1. In small bowl, combine **Soup,** water and parsley; set aside.

2. In medium bowl, combine ground beef, **Crumbs, Vegetable,** egg and **Herb.** Mix lightly, but well. Shape into 16 meatballs.

3. In 10-inch skillet over medium heat, in hot oil, cook meatballs until browned on all sides. Pour off fat. Stir soup mixture into skillet. Reduce heat to low. Cover; simmer 20 minutes. Makes 4 servings.

To Microwave: Use ingredients as above but omit oil. Prepare as above in Steps 1 and 2. In 12 by 8-inch microwave-safe baking dish, place meatballs; cover. Microwave on HIGH 4 to 5 minutes until almost done, turning over and rearranging meatballs once. Pour off fat. Stir soup mixture into dish; cover. Microwave on HIGH 4 to 6 minutes until heated through, stirring once.

Sausage and Peppers

1 pound Italian sausage, cut into 2-inch chunks
2 tablespoons water
2 large green peppers, cut into 1-inch-wide strips
1 medium onion, sliced and separated into rings
2 cloves garlic, minced
1 can (10½ to 11 ounces) condensed **Soup**
½ cup water
½ teaspoon **Herb,** crushed
Accompaniment

Soup	Herb	Accompaniment
Spanish style vegetable	oregano leaves	Italian bread
tomato bisque	basil leaves	polenta (see **Tip** below)
tomato	marjoram leaves	hot cooked spaghetti

1. In 10-inch covered skillet over medium heat, cook sausage and 2 tablespoons water 5 minutes. Uncover; cook until sausages are browned on all sides.

2. Add green peppers, onion and garlic; cook until vegetables are tender, stirring frequently.

3. Stir in **Soup,** ½ cup water and **Herb;** reduce heat to low. Cover; simmer 10 minutes. Serve with **Accompaniment.** Makes 4 servings.

Tip: *To prepare polenta: In heavy 4-quart saucepan, heat 4 cups water to boiling. With wire whisk, gradually stir in 1 cup cornmeal. Reduce heat to low. Simmer 20 to 25 minutes, stirring often. Pour into buttered 9-inch pie plate. Let stand 10 minutes; cut into wedges.*

Tacos

Meat
½ cup chopped onion
2 cloves garlic, minced
1 tablespoon chili powder
1 can (10½ to 11 ounces) condensed **Soup**
8 taco shells
1 cup shredded **Cheese**
Shredded lettuce
1 cup **Addition**

Meat	Soup	Cheese	Addition
1 pound ground beef	tomato	Cheddar	chopped tomatoes
1 pound ground pork	tomato rice	longhorn	diced avocado
1½ cups chopped cooked beef plus 2 tablespoons salad oil	Spanish style vegetable	Monterey Jack	chopped green onions
1 pound bulk pork sausage	tomato bisque	American	salsa

1. Preheat oven to 350°F. In 10-inch skillet over medium heat, cook **Meat,** onion, garlic and chili powder until meat is well browned, stirring to break up meat. Pour off fat. Stir in **Soup.** Heat through, stirring occasionally.

2. Place about ¼ cup meat mixture in each taco shell. Place on baking sheet. Bake 5 minutes. Top with **Cheese,** lettuce and **Addition.** Makes 8 tacos, 4 servings.

To Microwave: In 1½-quart microwave-safe casserole, crumble **Meat.** Add onion, garlic and chili powder; cover. Microwave on HIGH 6 to 8 minutes until meat is nearly done, stirring occasionally. Pour off fat. Stir in **Soup;** cover. Microwave on HIGH 2 to 3 minutes until heated through, stirring once. Place about ¼ cup meat mixture in each taco shell. In 12 by 8-inch microwave-safe dish, arrange taco shells. Microwave on HIGH 2 to 3 minutes. Top with **Cheese,** lettuce and **Addition.**

Best-Ever Meat Loaf

1 can (10¾ to 11 ounces) condensed **Soup**
Meat
Crumbs
1 egg, beaten
⅓ cup finely chopped onion
Seasoning
⅓ cup water

Soup	Meat	Crumbs	Seasoning
golden mushroom	2 pounds ground beef	½ cup fine dry bread crumbs	1 tablespoon Worcestershire
cream of mushroom	2 pounds meat loaf mix (beef, pork, veal)	½ cup quick-cooking oats	1 tablespoon soy sauce
Cheddar cheese	1½ pounds ground beef plus ½ pound Italian sausage, casings removed	½ cup finely crushed saltines	¼ cup chopped pimento-stuffed olives

1. In large bowl, thoroughly mix ½ cup of the **Soup, Meat, Crumbs,** egg, onion and **Seasoning.** In 12 by 8-inch baking pan, firmly shape meat into 8 by 4-inch loaf.

2. Bake at 350°F. 1¼ hours or until done. Remove meat loaf to platter; keep warm.

3. Pour off all but 3 tablespoons drippings from pan. Stir remaining **Soup** and water into drippings in pan, scraping up brown bits from bottom. Over medium heat, heat soup mixture until hot, stirring constantly. Serve gravy with meat loaf. Makes 8 servings.

Tip: *If using glass baking dish, remove drippings to saucepan to make gravy.*

Miniature Meat Loaves

1½ pounds ground beef
1 can (10½ ounces) condensed **Soup**
Crumbs
½ cup chopped onion
⅓ cup **Vegetable**
2 tablespoons chopped fresh parsley
Herb, crushed
¼ teaspoon pepper

Soup	Crumbs	Vegetable	Herb
vegetarian vegetable	2 cups soft whole wheat bread crumbs	chopped green pepper	1 teaspoon summer savory leaves
minestrone	1 cup fine dry bread crumbs	shredded carrot	1 teaspoon oregano leaves
Spanish style vegetable	2 cups soft white bread crumbs	chopped celery	½ teaspoon thyme leaves

1. In large bowl, thoroughly mix all ingredients. Firmly shape mixture into 6 small meat loaves. Place loaves in 15 by 10-inch jelly-roll pan.

2. Bake at 375°F. 40 minutes or until browned. Makes 6 servings.

To Microwave: Use ingredients as above but substitute 1 cup fine dry bread crumbs for **Crumbs** in all variations. Combine all ingredients as directed in Step 1. Firmly press mixture into six 5-ounce microwave-safe custard cups. Arrange custard cups in a ring in microwave oven. Microwave on HIGH 15 to 18 minutes until firm to the touch, rearranging once. Let stand 5 to 7 minutes.

Souper Enchiladas

½ cup salad oil
8 corn tortillas (6-inch)
1 cup chopped onion
1 large clove garlic, minced
1 can (11 to 11½ ounces) condensed **Soup**
2 cups shredded cooked **Meat**
½ cup water
1 teaspoon ground cumin
Seasoning
1 jar (8 ounces) taco sauce
1 cup shredded **Cheese**

Soup	Meat	Seasoning	Cheese
black bean	chicken	1 can (4 ounces) chopped green chilies, drained	Cheddar
bean with bacon	pork	2 jalapeño peppers, seeded and chopped	longhorn
chili beef	beef	¼ teaspoon hot pepper sauce	Monterey Jack

1. In 8-inch skillet over medium heat, in hot oil, fry tortillas, one at a time, 2 to 3 seconds on each side. Drain tortillas on paper towels.

2. Spoon about 2 tablespoons of the hot oil into 10-inch skillet. Over medium heat, in the 2 tablespoons oil, cook onion and garlic until tender, stirring occasionally. Stir in **Soup, Meat,** water, cumin and **Seasoning.** Heat through.

3. Spoon about ⅓ cup soup mixture onto each tortilla; roll up. Arrange filled tortillas in 12 by 8-inch baking dish. Pour taco sauce evenly over enchiladas. Sprinkle with **Cheese.** Cover with foil.

4. Bake at 350°F. 25 minutes. Uncover; bake 5 minutes more. Makes 4 servings.

To Microwave: Use ingredients as above but use only 1 tablespoon oil. In 2-quart microwave-safe casserole, combine only 1 tablespoon oil, onion and garlic; cover. Microwave on HIGH 2 to 3 minutes until tender. Stir in **Soup, Meat,** water, cumin and **Seasoning;** cover. Microwave on HIGH 4 to 6 minutes until heated through, stirring once. Let stand, covered. Meanwhile, wrap tortillas in paper towel and place in microwave oven. Microwave on HIGH 2 minutes or until tortillas are pliable. Assemble as in Step 3, placing filled tortillas in 12 by 8-inch microwave-safe dish. Pour taco sauce evenly over enchiladas; cover. Microwave on HIGH 8 to 10 minutes until hot, rotating dish once. Sprinkle with **Cheese.** Microwave on HIGH 2 to 3 minutes until cheese is melted.

Chimichangas

1 pound ground beef
1 medium onion, chopped
1 clove garlic, minced
1 can (10¾ to 11¼ ounces) condensed **Soup**
1 can (4 ounces) chopped green chilies, drained
1 tablespoon vinegar
1 teaspoon **Seasoning**
½ teaspoon ground cumin
8 flour tortillas (8-inch)
1 cup shredded **Cheese**
Salad oil
Shredded lettuce
Topping

Soup	Seasoning	Cheese	Topping
tomato bisque	oregano leaves, crushed	Monterey Jack	taco sauce
tomato rice	chili powder	American	chopped green onions
tomato	marjoram leaves, crushed	Provolone	chopped radishes
chili beef plus ½ cup water	basil leaves, crushed	longhorn	sour cream

1. In 10-inch skillet over medium heat, cook ground beef, onion and garlic until browned, stirring occasionally to break up meat. Pour off fat. Stir in **Soup,** chilies, vinegar, **Seasoning** and cumin; reduce heat. Simmer 10 to 15 minutes or until most of liquid evaporates. Remove from heat; cool slightly.

2. Spoon ¼ cup filling down center of one tortilla. Top with 2 tablespoons **Cheese.** Fold in sides of tortilla; roll up tortilla around filling. Secure with a toothpick. Assemble 2 or 3 at a time.

3. In 10-inch skillet, heat 1 inch oil to 350°F. Fry chimichangas 2 minutes or until golden, turning once. Remove and drain on paper towels. Garnish with lettuce and **Topping.** Makes 8 servings.

Tip: *To make burritos, prepare filling as above in Step 1. Spoon ¼ cup filling down center of one tortilla; top with 2 tablespoons* **Cheese.** *Roll tortilla around filling. Repeat with remaining tortillas and filling. Place on baking sheet; cover with foil. Bake at 350°F. 15 minutes until hot. Garnish as above.*

Tostadas

1 can (11¼ ounces) condensed chili beef soup
1 cup finely chopped cooked **Meat**
1 package (3 ounces) cream cheese, cubed
½ teaspoon oregano leaves, crushed
¼ cup water
Salad oil
6 corn tortillas (6-inch)
Shredded lettuce
Diced tomato
1 cup shredded **Cheese**
⅓ cup **Topping**
Taco sauce
Garnish

Meat	Cheese	Topping	Garnish
chicken	Monterey Jack	sour cream	sliced pitted ripe olives
beef	Monterey Jack with jalapeño peppers	plain yogurt	chopped green onions
pork	Cheddar	guacamole	chopped cilantro or parsley
ham	Muenster	creamy blue cheese dressing	pickled peppers

1. In 2-quart saucepan over low heat, heat soup, **Meat,** cream cheese, oregano and water until hot, stirring occasionally.

2. In small skillet over medium heat, heat ½ inch oil to 350°F. Fry tortillas, one at a time, until golden brown, turning once (about 1 minute). Remove and drain on paper towels.

3. Top each tostada shell with ¼ cup of the soup mixture. Top with lettuce, tomato, **Cheese, Topping** and taco sauce. Sprinkle with **Garnish.** Makes 6 servings.

Tip: *Prepared tostada shells are available at your grocer—just heat and top with filling and toppings.*

To Microwave: Prepare tostada shells as in Step 2. While shells are draining, in 1½-quart microwave-safe casserole, combine soup, **Meat,** cream cheese, oregano and water; cover. Microwave on HIGH 5 to 8 minutes until hot, stirring occasionally. Proceed as in Step 3.

Rice Pizza

3 cups cooked rice (about 1 cup raw)
2 cups shredded **Cheese**
2 eggs, beaten
½ pound bulk pork sausage
1 can (10¾ ounces) condensed tomato soup
¼ teaspoon **Seasoning**
Vegetable
Topper
¼ cup grated Romano cheese

Cheese	Seasoning	Vegetable	Topper
sharp Cheddar	oregano leaves, crushed	1 medium zucchini, sliced	¼ cup sliced pimento-stuffed olives
mozzarella	marjoram leaves, crushed	1 cup sliced mushrooms	¼ cup chopped green pepper
Monterey Jack	chili powder	1 cup fresh or frozen whole kernel corn	2 tablespoons finely chopped drained green chilies
colby	Italian seasoning, crushed	1 medium onion, sliced and separated into rings	1 can (2 ounces) anchovy fillets, drained

1. Grease 12-inch pizza pan. Preheat oven to 450°F.

2. In medium bowl, combine rice, ¾ cup of the **Cheese** and eggs; mix well. Pat mixture evenly onto prepared pizza pan, building up ½-inch rim. Bake 15 minutes or until crust is set.

3. Meanwhile, in 10-inch skillet over medium heat, cook sausage until browned, stirring to break up meat. Remove sausage from pan; drain on paper towels.

4. In small bowl, stir together soup and **Seasoning.** Spread over baked crust. Arrange **Vegetable,** cooked sausage, **Topper,** remaining 1¼ cups **Cheese** and Romano cheese over soup.

5. Bake 15 minutes or until crust is golden brown and cheese is melted. Makes 6 servings.

Quick Stovetop Supper

1 tablespoon butter or margarine
½ cup sliced mushrooms
¼ cup chopped onion
1 can (10¾ to 11 ounces) condensed **Soup**
½ cup milk
½ teaspoon dry mustard
Meat
½ cup **Vegetable**
Accompaniment

Soup	Meat	Vegetable	Accompaniment
cream of mushroom	4 ounces dried beef, rinsed and cut into strips	drained, cooked peas	toast points
cream of celery	1 cup cooked ham cut into strips	drained, cooked cut green beans	baked potatoes, split
cream of chicken	1 cup cooked turkey cut into strips	drained, cooked diced carrots	hot cooked noodles
Cheddar cheese	1 can (about 7 ounces) tuna, drained and flaked	packed chopped raw spinach	baked patty shells

1. In 2-quart saucepan over medium heat, in hot butter, cook mushrooms and onion until tender, stirring occasionally.

2. Stir in **Soup,** milk and mustard until smooth. Stir in **Meat** and **Vegetable.** Heat through, stirring occasionally. Serve over **Accompaniment.** Makes about 2 cups, 4 servings.

To Microwave: In 2-quart microwave-safe casserole, combine butter, mushrooms and onion; cover. Microwave on HIGH 3 to 4 minutes until onion is tender, stirring once. Stir in **Soup,** milk and mustard until smooth. Stir in **Meat** and **Vegetable;** cover. Microwave on HIGH 5 to 6 minutes until heated through, stirring occasionally. Serve over **Accompaniment.**

Supper à la King

¼ cup butter or margarine
½ cup diced green pepper
⅓ cup chopped onion
1 can (10¾ ounces) condensed **Soup**
¾ cup milk
2 cups cubed cooked **Meat**
¾ cup shredded **Cheese**
¼ cup diced pimento
Accompaniment

Soup	Meat	Cheese	Accompaniment
cream of chicken	chicken	Swiss	shredded zucchini, cooked and drained
cream of asparagus	ham	Cheddar	baked potatoes, split
cream of mushroom	turkey	Muenster	cooked spaghetti squash (see **Tip** below)
cream of celery	kielbasa	American	biscuits, split

1. In 10-inch skillet over medium heat, in hot butter, cook green pepper and onion until tender, stirring occasionally. Stir in **Soup** and milk; blend well. Stir in **Meat, Cheese** and pimento. Cook 5 minutes more or until heated through.

2. Arrange **Accompaniment** on serving platter. Serve sauce over accompaniment. Makes about 3½ cups sauce, 6 servings.

Tip: *To cook spaghetti squash: Halve squash lengthwise; remove seeds and stringy portions. In 10-inch skillet, place squash halves cut side up. Add 1 inch water. Over medium heat, heat to boiling. Reduce heat to low. Cover; simmer 30 minutes or until fork-tender. Drain. With fork, scrape spaghetti-like strands from squash shell; place on serving platter. Discard shells.*

To Microwave: Use ingredients as above but use only 2 tablespoons butter. In 2-quart microwave-safe casserole, combine only 2 tablespoons butter, green pepper and onion; cover. Microwave on HIGH 2 to 3 minutes until vegetables are tender. Stir in **Soup** and milk; blend well. Stir in **Meat, Cheese** and pimento; cover. Microwave on HIGH 7 to 9 minutes until heated through, stirring occasionally. Serve as above.

Creamy Noodle Supper

2 tablespoons butter or margarine
⅓ cup chopped onion
1 can (10¾ ounces) condensed **Soup**
½ cup milk
⅛ teaspoon rubbed sage
⅛ teaspoon pepper
4 ounces (about 3 cups) medium noodles, cooked and drained
Meat
1 cup drained, cooked **Vegetable**
Topping

Soup	Meat	Vegetable	Topping
cream of chicken	1½ cups diced cooked chicken	mixed vegetables	2 tablespoons buttered bread crumbs
cream of shrimp	1 can (about 7 ounces) tuna, drained and flaked	diced carrots	¼ cup toasted sliced almonds
cream of mushroom	1½ cups diced cooked ham	peas	½ cup shredded American cheese
cream of onion	1½ cups diced cooked beef	cut green beans	½ cup crushed potato chips

1. In 3-quart saucepan over medium heat, in hot butter, cook onion until tender, stirring often. Stir in **Soup,** milk, sage and pepper until well mixed. Stir in noodles, **Meat** and **Vegetable** just until mixed. Turn into 1½-quart casserole.

2. Bake at 400°F. 20 minutes or until hot. Stir casserole; sprinkle with **Topping.** Bake 5 minutes more. Makes 4 servings.

To Microwave: In 1½-quart microwave-safe casserole, combine butter, onion and **Vegetable;** cover. Microwave on HIGH 3 to 5 minutes until onion is tender, stirring once. Stir in **Soup,** milk, sage and pepper until well mixed. Stir in noodles and **Meat;** cover. Microwave on HIGH 6 to 8 minutes until hot, stirring once. Sprinkle with **Topping.** Microwave, uncovered, on HIGH 2 minutes more.

Curried Noodle Pie

1 can (10¾ ounces) condensed **Soup**
1 cup sour cream
4 ounces (about 3 cups) medium noodles, cooked and drained
1 egg, beaten
2 tablespoons salad oil
1 clove garlic, minced
1 teaspoon curry powder
Meat
1 cup drained, cooked **Vegetable**
Garnish

Soup	Meat	Vegetable	Garnish
cream of onion	3 cups diced cooked chicken	sliced carrots	toasted sliced almonds
cream of chicken	3 cups diced cooked pork	mixed vegetables	sliced green onions
cream of mushroom	3 cups diced cooked beef	lima beans	toasted flaked coconut
golden mushroom	2 cans (about 7 ounces each) tuna, drained and flaked	cut asparagus	diced pimento

1. Grease 9-inch pie plate. In medium bowl, stir together **Soup** and sour cream. In large bowl, stir ¾ cup of the soup mixture into noodles, stir in egg, mixing well. Press noodles into bottom and up side of prepared pie plate to form crust; set aside.

2. In 10-inch skillet over medium heat, in hot oil, cook garlic and curry powder 1 minute. Stir in remaining soup mixture, **Meat** and **Vegetable.** Arrange in noodle crust. Cover with foil.

3. Bake at 350°F. 30 minutes or until hot. Sprinkle with **Garnish.** Let stand 10 minutes before cutting into wedges. Makes 6 servings.

Stuffed Cabbage Leaves

1 pound **Meat**
½ cup chopped onion
1 can (10½ ounces) condensed beef broth
½ cup **Grain**
½ teaspoon grated lemon peel
½ cup **Fruit**
¼ cup chopped walnuts
¼ cup chopped fresh parsley
½ teaspoon dried mint leaves (optional)
1 medium head cabbage
1 can (10½ to 11 ounces) condensed **Soup**
¼ teaspoon ground cinnamon

Meat	Grain	Fruit	Soup
ground pork	raw bulgur wheat	chopped apple	tomato plus 1 tablespoon lemon juice
ground lamb	raw brown rice	golden raisins	Spanish style vegetable
ground beef	raw regular rice	chopped dried apricots	tomato rice plus 1 tablespoon lemon juice

1. In 10-inch skillet over medium heat, cook **Meat** and onion until meat is well browned, stirring occasionally to break up meat. Pour off fat.

2. Add beef broth, **Grain** and lemon peel. Heat to boiling. Reduce heat to low. Cover; simmer until grain is tender, about 45 minutes for brown rice or 20 to 25 minutes for regular rice or bulgur; add a little water during cooking if mixture becomes dry. Remove from heat. Stir in **Fruit,** walnuts, parsley and mint.

3. Meanwhile, in 4-quart saucepan over high heat, heat about 6 cups water to boiling. Add whole head of cabbage to boiling water. Reduce heat to low. Cover; simmer 1 to 2 minutes or until outer leaves are softened. Remove cabbage from water. Carefully remove 6 outer leaves. Reserve remaining cabbage for another use.

4. Drain cabbage leaves on paper towels. Lay leaves flat on cutting board and cut out any tough stems. Spoon about ¾ cup meat filling into center of one leaf. Fold in sides, then roll up from stem end to form a bundle. Repeat with remaining leaves and filling.

5. In medium bowl, stir together **Soup** and cinnamon. Pour ½ of the soup mixture into 12 by 8-inch baking dish. Place cabbage rolls seam side down in prepared dish. Pour remaining soup mixture over all. Cover with foil. Bake at 350°F. 35 minutes or until heated through. Makes 6 servings.

Cheesy Rice Bake

1 can (10¾ to 11 ounces) condensed **Soup**
⅓ cup milk
1 tablespoon chopped fresh parsley
2 cups cooked rice (about ⅔ cup raw)
Protein
1 cup **Vegetable**
Cheese

Soup	Protein	Vegetable	Cheese
cream of mushroom	1 can (15 ounces) salmon, drained and flaked	drained, cooked peas	1 cup shredded sharp Cheddar
tomato	2 cups diced cooked beef	drained, cooked whole kernel corn	1 cup shredded mozzarella
Cheddar cheese	2 cups diced cooked ham	drained, cooked chopped spinach	¼ cup grated Parmesan
cream of onion	1 can (16 ounces) kidney beans, drained	chopped tomato	1 cup shredded longhorn

1. In large bowl, combine **Soup,** milk and parsley; stir to blend. Stir in rice, **Protein** and **Vegetable.** Turn mixture into 10 by 6-inch baking dish; sprinkle with **Cheese.**

2. Bake at 350°F. 30 minutes or until heated through. Makes about 7 cups, 6 servings.

To Microwave: Prepare as in Step 1, but turn rice mixture into 10 by 6-inch microwave-safe dish; cover. Microwave on HIGH 7 to 10 minutes until heated through, stirring once. Sprinkle with **Cheese.** Microwave on HIGH 2 minutes or until cheese is melted.

Chicken-Stuffing Bake

1 cup water
¼ cup butter or margarine
1 package (7 ounces) seasoned stuffing mix
1 can (10¾ to 11 ounces) condensed **Soup**
½ cup mayonnaise
⅓ cup milk
2 cups diced cooked chicken or turkey
2 stalks celery, chopped
1 cup drained, cooked **Vegetable**
½ teaspoon **Seasoning**
Cheese

Soup	Vegetable	Seasoning	Cheese
cream of chicken	peas	thyme leaves, crushed	1 cup shredded Cheddar
cream of mushroom	mixed vegetables	marjoram leaves, crushed	1 cup shredded Swiss
cream of onion	chopped spinach	rubbed sage	1 cup shredded Monterey Jack
Cheddar cheese	chopped broccoli	poultry seasoning	¼ cup grated Parmesan

1. In 1-quart saucepan over high heat, heat water and butter to boiling. In large bowl, pour hot water mixture over stuffing mix; toss to mix well. Pat ½ of the stuffing mixture into 12 by 8-inch baking dish.

2. In medium bowl, stir together **Soup,** mayonnaise, milk, chicken, celery, **Vegetable** and **Seasoning** until well mixed. Spoon evenly over stuffing mixture in baking dish; top with remaining stuffing mixture.

3. Bake at 400°F. 30 minutes or until heated through. Sprinkle with **Cheese.** Bake 5 minutes more or until cheese is melted. Makes 6 servings.

To Microwave: Prepare as in Steps 1 and 2 but assemble in 12 by 8-inch microwave-safe dish; cover. Microwave on HIGH 8 to 10 minutes until heated through, rotating dish once. Sprinkle with **Cheese.** Microwave on HIGH 2 minutes or until cheese is melted.

Souper Easy Quiche

4 eggs
1 can (10¾ to 11 ounces) condensed **Soup**
½ cup light cream
1 cup shredded **Cheese**
Meat
½ cup **Vegetable**
1 9-inch unbaked piecrust
Ground nutmeg

Soup	Cheese	Meat	Vegetable
Cheddar cheese	sharp Cheddar	½ cup diced cooked ham	drained, cooked chopped broccoli
cream of mushroom	American	6 slices bacon, cooked, drained and crumbled	drained, cooked cut asparagus
cream of onion	Monterey Jack	½ cup diced cooked chicken	sliced mushrooms
cream of celery	Swiss	½ cup diced cooked turkey	drained, cooked chopped spinach

1. In medium bowl, beat eggs until foamy. Gradually add **Soup** and cream, mixing well.

2. Sprinkle **Cheese, Meat** and **Vegetable** evenly over piecrust. Pour soup mixture over all. Sprinkle with nutmeg.

3. Bake at 350°F. 50 minutes or until center is set. Let stand 10 minutes before serving. Makes 6 servings.

Eggs Goldenrod

1 can (10¾ ounces) condensed **Soup**
½ cup **Liquid**
2 tablespoons chopped fresh parsley
¼ teaspoon dry mustard
4 hard-cooked eggs
Bread

Soup	Liquid	Bread
cream of celery	milk	4 slices toast
cream of chicken	chicken broth	4 English muffins, split and toasted
cream of onion	light cream	4 squares hot corn bread
cream of mushroom	water	4 biscuits, split

1. In small saucepan, stir together **Soup, Liquid,** parsley and mustard until smooth.

2. Separate egg yolks and whites. Chop whites coarsely; add to soup mixture. Over medium heat, heat through, stirring occasionally.

3. Meanwhile, force egg yolks through sieve. Serve egg mixture on **Bread,** using about ½ cup per serving; garnish with sieved yolks. Makes about 2 cups, 4 servings.

Tip: *Make this dish a little more special by sprinkling it with fresh alfalfa sprouts.*

To Microwave: In 1½-quart microwave-safe casserole, stir together **Soup, Liquid,** parsley and mustard; cover. Microwave on HIGH 2 to 3 minutes until hot, stirring once. Meanwhile, separate eggs and chop whites as in Step 2. Add whites to soup mixture; cover. Microwave on HIGH 1 to 2 minutes until heated through; stir. Serve as in Step 3.

Versatile Crepes

3 eggs
1 cup milk
⅔ cup all-purpose flour
1 can (10¾ to 11 ounces) condensed **Soup**
Liquid
1½ cups shredded **Cheese**
Filling

Soup	Liquid	Cheese	Filling
cream of chicken	2 tablespoons dry sherry plus ⅓ cup water	sharp Cheddar	2 cups diced cooked chicken
cream of mushroom	½ cup milk	longhorn	1 can (15 ounces) salmon, drained and flaked
Cheddar cheese	¼ cup dry white wine plus ¼ cup water	Swiss	2 cups diced cooked ham
cream of onion	½ cup light cream	Monterey Jack	2 cups drained, cooked chopped broccoli

1. In medium bowl, combine eggs, milk and flour; beat until smooth.

2. Over medium heat, heat 8-inch crepe pan or skillet. When hot, brush lightly with salad oil. Add scant ¼ cup batter to skillet, rotating pan to spread batter evenly. Cook until surface is dry and edges are browned. Turn over; cook other side a few seconds. Remove from pan, stacking crepes as they are made. Repeat to make 10 crepes, brushing pan with oil as needed.

3. In 2-quart saucepan over medium heat, heat **Soup** and **Liquid,** stirring to mix well. Add 1 cup of the **Cheese,** stirring until cheese melts. Stir 1 cup of the sauce into **Filling.** Spoon about 3 tablespoons filling mixture down center of each crepe. Roll up. Repeat with remaining crepes.

4. Arrange rolled crepes seam side down in 12 by 8-inch baking dish. Pour remaining sauce over all; sprinkle with remaining ½ cup **Cheese.** Cover. Bake at 350°F. 25 minutes or until heated through. Makes 5 servings.

To Microwave: Prepare crepes as above in Steps 1 and 2. In 1-quart microwave-safe casserole, combine **Soup** and **Liquid,** stirring well. Add 1 cup of the **Cheese;** cover. Microwave on HIGH 4 to 6 minutes until cheese melts, stirring occasionally. Stir 1 cup sauce into **Filling.** Fill and roll crepes as directed. Arrange rolled crepes in 12 by 8-inch microwave-safe dish. Pour remaining sauce over all; cover. Microwave on HIGH 7 to 9 minutes until hot, rotating dish once. Sprinkle with remaining ½ cup **Cheese.** Microwave on HIGH 2 minutes or until cheese is melted.

Easy Soufflé

1 can (10½ to 11 ounces) condensed **Soup**
1 cup shredded **Cheese**
Seasoning
6 eggs, separated

Soup	Cheese	Seasoning
Cheddar cheese	sharp Cheddar	dash cayenne pepper
cream of asparagus	Swiss	⅛ teaspoon ground nutmeg
tomato	American	¼ teaspoon marjoram leaves, crushed
cream of chicken	Jarlsberg	2 tablespoons chopped fresh parsley

1. In 1-quart saucepan, combine **Soup, Cheese** and **Seasoning.** Over low heat, heat until cheese melts, stirring occasionally. Remove from heat.

2. In large bowl with mixer at high speed, beat egg whites until stiff peaks form; set aside. In small bowl with mixer at high speed, beat egg yolks until thick and lemon-colored. Gradually stir in soup mixture; fold into egg whites.

3. Pour into ungreased 2-quart casserole or soufflé dish. Bake at 300°F. 1 hour or until soufflé is lightly browned. Serve immediately. Makes 6 servings.

Cheese Omelet Roll

1 can (10¾ to 11 ounces) condensed **Soup**
6 eggs, separated
¼ teaspoon cream of tartar
2 cups shredded **Cheese**
Meat
1 cup **Vegetable**

Soup	Cheese	Meat	Vegetable
cream of celery	Swiss	½ pound bacon, cooked, drained and crumbled	finely chopped raw spinach
cream of chicken	Monterey Jack	½ pound bulk pork sausage, cooked, drained and crumbled	drained, cooked chopped broccoli
Cheddar cheese	Cheddar	1 cup diced cooked ham	drained, cooked chopped asparagus

1. Preheat oven to 350°F. Oil 15 by 10-inch jelly-roll pan; line with aluminum foil, extending 3 inches beyond pan on each end. Oil and flour bottom and sides of foil.

2. In 1-quart saucepan over medium heat, heat **Soup,** stirring occasionally. Remove from heat. In small bowl with fork, beat egg yolks. Stir some of hot soup into yolks, then return to soup. Over low heat, cook 1 minute, stirring constantly. Remove from heat.

3. In large bowl with mixer at high speed, beat egg whites and cream of tartar until stiff peaks form. Fold soup mixture into whites. Fold in 1 cup of the **Cheese.** Spread in prepared pan. Bake 20 to 25 minutes until puffy and browned.

4. Invert onto waxed paper; gently remove foil (some omelet may stick to foil). Sprinkle with remaining 1 cup **Cheese, Meat** and **Vegetable.** With aid of waxed paper, roll up jelly-roll fashion, starting at narrow side. Roll onto serving plate. Makes 6 servings.

Tip: *Omelet is delicious served plain or with a cheese or tomato sauce.*

Main Dish Spoonbread

Meat
Vegetable
1 cup cornmeal
1¼ cups water
3 tablespoons butter or margarine
1 can (10¾ to 11 ounces) condensed **Soup**
3 eggs, beaten
1 teaspoon baking powder
Seasoning
Syrup or butter

Meat	Vegetable	Soup	Seasoning
6 slices bacon, diced	¼ cup finely chopped onion	Cheddar cheese	dash cayenne pepper
1 cup diced cooked ham plus 2 tablespoons butter or margarine	¼ cup chopped green pepper	cream of chicken	⅛ teaspoon paprika
½ pound bulk pork sausage	½ cup finely chopped celery	cream of onion	½ teaspoon rubbed sage
1 cup diced cooked corned beef plus 2 tablespoons salad oil	½ cup chopped mushrooms	cream of mushroom	⅛ teaspoon garlic powder

1. Butter 2-quart casserole.

2. In 3-quart saucepan over medium heat, cook **Meat** until browned, stirring occasionally. With slotted spoon, remove meat from pan; drain on paper towels. In drippings, cook **Vegetable** until tender.

3. Stir in cornmeal and water until smooth. Heat to boiling, stirring constantly. Remove from heat.

4. Stir in butter until melted. Stir in **Soup,** eggs, baking powder, **Seasoning** and reserved meat. Pour into prepared casserole.

5. Bake at 350°F. 50 minutes or until knife inserted in center comes out clean. Serve with syrup or butter. Makes 6 servings.

Vegetable Lasagna

2 tablespoons olive or salad oil
1 large onion, chopped
1 clove garlic, minced
1 teaspoon Italian seasoning, crushed
Vegetable
1 can (10¾ to 11 ounces) condensed **Soup**
Cheese
1 egg
1 jar (32 ounces) spaghetti sauce
Liquid
9 lasagna noodles, cooked and drained
2 cups shredded mozzarella cheese

Vegetable	Soup	Cheese	Liquid
2 packages (10 ounces each) frozen chopped broccoli, thawed and drained	cream of chicken	2 cups shredded sharp Cheddar	½ cup dry red wine
2 packages (10 ounces each) frozen chopped spinach, thawed and drained	cream of mushroom	1 cup grated Parmesan	1 cup heavy cream
4 cups sliced zucchini	cream of celery	2 cups shredded Swiss	2 tablespoons vinegar plus ½ cup water
2 packages (9 ounces each) frozen cut green beans, thawed and drained	Cheddar cheese	1 cup ricotta plus ¼ cup crumbled blue cheese	½ cup plain yogurt

1. In 10-inch skillet over medium heat, in hot oil, cook onion, garlic and Italian seasoning until onion is tender, stirring occasionally. Stir in **Vegetable;** cook until vegetable is tender and liquid evaporates. Remove from heat; stir in **Soup, Cheese** and egg. Set filling aside.

2. In medium bowl, stir together spaghetti sauce and **Liquid;** pour ½ of the sauce mixture into 13 by 9-inch baking dish. Set remainder aside.

3. Arrange 3 lasagna noodles over sauce; spread with ½ of the vegetable filling. Sprinkle with ⅓ of the mozzarella. Arrange 3 more noodles over cheese; spread with remaining filling. Sprinkle with another ⅓ of the mozzarella. Top with remaining 3 noodles and remaining sauce.

4. Bake at 350°F. 40 minutes or until hot. Sprinkle with remaining ⅓ of the mozzarella; bake 5 minutes more. Let stand 15 minutes before serving. Makes 6 servings.

Lasagna Roll-Ups

1 pound **Meat**
1 cup chopped onion
2 cloves garlic, minced
1 tablespoon **Herb,** crushed
1 can (10¾ ounces) condensed tomato soup
1 cup water
1 can (6 ounces) tomato paste
1½ pounds ricotta cheese
1 cup shredded **Cheese 1**
2 tablespoons chopped fresh parsley
¼ teaspoon ground nutmeg
8 lasagna noodles, cooked and drained
¼ cup grated **Cheese 2**

Meat	Herb	Cheese 1	Cheese 2
Italian sausage, casings removed	oregano leaves	mozzarella	Parmesan
ground pork	basil leaves	longhorn	Romano
ground beef	marjoram leaves	Provolone	Gruyère

1. To make sauce, in 4-quart Dutch oven over medium heat, cook **Meat,** onion, garlic and **Herb** until meat is browned and onion is tender, stirring to break up meat. Pour off fat. Stir in soup, water and tomato paste. Heat to boiling; reduce heat to low. Simmer, uncovered, 30 minutes or until desired consistency, stirring occasionally.

2. To make filling, in large bowl, combine ricotta cheese, **Cheese 1,** parsley and nutmeg; set aside.

3. Pat drained noodles dry with paper towels. On each noodle, spread about ⅓ cup cheese filling. Fold over 1 inch and roll up each noodle jelly-roll fashion.

4. Spread 2 cups of the meat sauce in 13 by 9-inch baking dish. Place rolls seam side down in dish. Spoon remaining sauce over rolls. Sprinkle with **Cheese 2.** Bake at 350°F. 45 minutes or until hot. Let stand 5 minutes before serving. Makes 8 servings.

To Microwave: Use ingredients as above but use only ½ cup water. To make sauce, in 2-quart microwave-safe casserole, crumble **Meat.** Add onion, garlic and **Herb;** cover. Microwave on HIGH 6 to 8 minutes until meat is done and onion is tender, stirring occasionally. Pour off fat. Stir in soup, only ½ cup water and tomato paste; cover. Microwave on HIGH 5 to 7 minutes until boiling, stirring once. Proceed as in Steps 2 and 3. Spread 2 cups of the sauce in 12 by 8-inch microwave-safe dish. Assemble sauce and rolls as in Step 4; cover. Microwave on HIGH 12 to 15 minutes until heated through, rotating dish twice. Let stand, covered, 5 minutes before serving.

Baked Manicotti

2 tablespoons salad oil
½ cup finely chopped onion
1 clove garlic, minced
½ teaspoon **Herb,** crushed
1 can (10¾ to 11¼ ounces) condensed **Soup**
1 soup can water
Tomatoes
Flavoring
1 small bay leaf
1 container (15 ounces) ricotta cheese
1 cup shredded mozzarella cheese
½ cup grated Parmesan cheese
1 egg
1 tablespoon chopped fresh parsley
10 manicotti shells, cooked and drained

Herb	Soup	Tomatoes	Flavoring
basil leaves	tomato	1 can (6 ounces) tomato paste	2 tablespoons grated Parmesan cheese
oregano leaves	tomato bisque	1 can (8 ounces) tomato sauce	¼ cup chopped green pepper
marjoram leaves	chili beef	½ cup ketchup	⅛ teaspoon ground cloves

1. To make sauce, in 3-quart saucepan over medium heat, in hot oil, cook onion, garlic and **Herb** until onion is tender. Stir in **Soup,** water, **Tomatoes, Flavoring** and bay leaf. Heat to boiling; reduce heat. Simmer, uncovered, 30 minutes or until desired consistency, stirring occasionally. Discard bay leaf.

2. To make filling, in medium bowl, combine ricotta, mozzarella, ¼ cup of the Parmesan, egg and parsley; stir to mix well. Using spoon or pastry bag, fill each manicotti shell with ¼ cup of the cheese filling.

3. Spoon 1 cup of the sauce into 12 by 8-inch baking dish; arrange manicotti over sauce. Top with remaining sauce and remaining ¼ cup Parmesan cheese. Bake at 350°F. 30 minutes or until hot. Makes 5 servings.

To Microwave: Use ingredients as above but use only ½ soup can water. In 2-quart microwave-safe casserole, combine oil, onion, garlic and **Herb;** cover. Microwave on HIGH 2 to 3 minutes until onion is tender. Stir in **Soup,** only ½ soup can water, **Tomatoes, Flavoring** and bay leaf; cover. Microwave on HIGH 4 to 5 minutes until boiling; stir. Microwave, uncovered, on HIGH 6 to 8 minutes more until desired consistency is reached, stirring once. Discard bay leaf. Proceed as in Step 2. Spoon 1 cup sauce into 12 by 8-inch microwave-safe dish; arrange manicotti over sauce. Top with remaining sauce and remaining ¼ cup Parmesan cheese; cover. Microwave on HIGH 8 to 10 minutes until hot, rotating twice. Let stand, covered, 3 minutes.

Pasta with White Seafood Sauce

½ cup butter or margarine
½ cup salad or olive oil
4 cloves garlic, minced
1 can (10¾ ounces) condensed chicken broth
Herb
Seafood
12 ounces **Pasta,** cooked and drained
Grated Parmesan or Romano cheese

Herb	Seafood	Pasta
¼ cup chopped fresh parsley	1 can (6½ ounces) chopped clams	spaghetti
½ cup chopped fresh basil	1 can (6½ ounces) tuna packed in water	linguine
¼ cup chopped fresh chives	1 can (7 ounces) salmon	corkscrew macaroni
1 teaspoon oregano leaves, crushed	1 can (4½ ounces) shrimp, drained	medium noodles

1. In 3-quart saucepan over medium heat, in hot butter and oil, cook garlic until golden. Add broth and **Herb.** Heat to boiling; reduce heat to low. Simmer, uncovered, 10 minutes.

2. Add **Seafood** with its liquid (do not use shrimp liquid); simmer 2 minutes more, stirring gently to break up tuna or salmon. Serve sauce over hot cooked **Pasta.** Pass grated cheese. Makes 6 servings.

Pasta with Shrimp Sauce

¼ cup salad oil
2 cups sliced mushrooms
¾ cup chopped onion
2 cloves garlic, minced
½ pound medium shrimp, shelled and deveined
Seafood
1 can (10¾ to 11 ounces) condensed **Soup**
Liquid
¼ cup chopped fresh parsley
8 ounces **Pasta,** cooked and drained
Grated Parmesan cheese

Seafood	Soup	Liquid	Pasta
½ pound bay scallops	cream of mushroom	1 cup half-and-half	linguine
1 can (6½ ounces) minced clams, drained	cream of celery	¼ cup dry sherry plus ¼ cup milk	spaghetti
½ pound cod or other fish, cut into chunks	cream of shrimp	¼ cup dry white wine plus ¼ cup milk	medium noodles
½ pound additional shrimp	Cheddar cheese	1 cup tomato juice	small shell macaroni

1. In 10-inch skillet over medium heat, in hot oil, cook mushrooms, onion and garlic until tender, stirring occasionally. Add shrimp and **Seafood;** cook 2 minutes more until seafood is done, stirring constantly.

2. In medium bowl, combine **Soup** and **Liquid;** mix well. Stir into skillet; add parsley. Heat through but do not boil. Serve sauce over hot cooked **Pasta.** Pass grated Parmesan cheese. Makes 4 servings.

Vegetable-Stuffed Fish Rolls

½ cup chopped tomato
½ cup chopped mushrooms
¼ cup chopped green onions
1 can (10¾ to 11 ounces) condensed **Soup**
6 **Fish** fillets (1½ pounds)
¼ cup **Liquid**
1 cup shredded **Cheese**

Soup	Fish	Liquid	Cheese
cream of shrimp	flounder	dry sherry	Swiss
cream of mushroom	sole	dry white wine	Provolone
Cheddar cheese	perch	milk	sharp Cheddar
cream of celery	haddock	water	Muenster

1. In medium bowl, combine tomato, mushrooms, green onions and ¼ cup of the **Soup.** Place about 3 tablespoons of the mixture on each **Fish** fillet and roll up. Secure with toothpicks if needed. Place fish rolls seam side down in 10 by 6-inch baking dish. Bake at 350°F. 25 minutes or until fish flakes easily when tested with fork. Discard any liquid in baking dish.

2. Meanwhile, in 2-quart saucepan, combine remaining **Soup** and **Liquid.** Over medium heat, heat through. Pour sauce over fish rolls; sprinkle with **Cheese.**

3. Bake 2 minutes more or until cheese is melted. Makes 6 servings.

To Microwave: In medium bowl, combine tomato, mushrooms, green onions and ¼ cup of the **Soup.** Fill and roll **Fish** as directed. Place fish rolls seam side down in 10 by 6-inch microwave-safe dish; cover. Microwave on HIGH 8 to 14 minutes until fish flakes easily when tested with fork, rotating dish twice. Discard any liquid in dish. Let stand, covered, 2 to 3 minutes. Meanwhile, in 2-cup glass measure, combine remaining **Soup** and **Liquid.** Microwave on HIGH 2 minutes or until hot. Pour sauce over fish rolls; top with **Cheese.** Microwave on HIGH 1 minute more or until cheese is melted.

Fish-Vegetable Bake

1 package (10 ounces) frozen **Vegetable,** thawed and well drained
1½ pounds **Fish** steaks
1 small onion, thinly sliced and separated into rings
1 can (10¾ to 11 ounces) condensed **Soup**
1 tablespoon lemon juice
Seasoning
⅛ teaspoon pepper
1 medium tomato, sliced

Vegetable	Fish	Soup	Seasoning
chopped spinach	haddock	Cheddar cheese	¼ teaspoon oregano leaves, crushed
chopped broccoli	halibut	cream of mushroom	¼ cup grated Parmesan cheese
cut asparagus	salmon	cream of shrimp	½ teaspoon dill weed, crushed

1. In 9 by 9-inch baking dish, arrange **Vegetable.** Top with **Fish** steaks and sliced onion.

2. In small bowl, stir together **Soup,** lemon juice, **Seasoning** and pepper. Spoon over onion.

3. Bake at 350°F. 25 to 30 minutes until fish flakes easily with fork. Top with tomato slices. Bake 5 minutes more. Makes 4 servings.

Perfect Tuna Casserole

1 can (10¾ ounces) condensed **Soup**
¼ cup milk
1 can (about 7 ounces) tuna, drained and flaked
2 hard-cooked eggs, sliced
1 cup frozen **Vegetable,** cooked and drained
Topper

Soup	Vegetable	Topper
cream of mushroom	peas	½ cup coarsely crumbled potato chips
cream of onion	cut green beans	3 slices American cheese, cut into slivers
cream of shrimp	cut broccoli	¼ cup toasted sliced almonds
New England clam chowder	whole kernel corn	1 medium tomato, sliced

1. In 1-quart casserole, stir together **Soup** and milk until well mixed. Stir in tuna, eggs and **Vegetable.**

2. Bake at 350°F. 25 minutes or until hot; stir.

3. Garnish with **Topper;** bake 5 minutes more. Makes 4 servings.

To Microwave: In 1-quart microwave-safe casserole, stir together **Soup** and milk. Stir in tuna, eggs and **Vegetable;** cover. Microwave on HIGH 8 to 10 minutes until hot, stirring occasionally. Garnish with **Topper.** Microwave on HIGH 1 to 3 minutes more until heated through.

Salmon and Noodle Skillet

1 can (15 ounces) salmon, drained and flaked
1 can (10¾ to 11 ounces) condensed **Soup**
Crumbs
2 tablespoons finely chopped onion
2 tablespoons chopped fresh parsley
1 tablespoon lemon juice
1 egg, beaten
Vegetable
2 tablespoons butter or margarine
½ cup sour cream
½ cup milk
4 ounces (about 3 cups) medium noodles, cooked and drained
Seasoning

Soup	Crumbs	Vegetable	Seasoning
cream of celery	1 cup soft bread crumbs	2 cups fresh or frozen cut asparagus	½ teaspoon dill weed, crushed
cream of mushroom	½ cup finely crushed saltines	2 cups fresh or frozen cut green beans	½ teaspoon marjoram leaves, crushed
cream of chicken	½ cup fine dry bread crumbs	2 cups fresh or frozen cut broccoli	¼ teaspoon ground nutmeg
Cheddar cheese	¼ cup quick-cooking oats	1 cup fresh or frozen peas	2 tablespoons grated Parmesan cheese

1. In medium bowl, combine salmon, ¼ cup of the **Soup, Crumbs,** onion, parsley, lemon juice and egg; mix well. Shape into 4 patties, each about 1 inch thick.

2. In 10-inch skillet over medium heat, in ½ inch boiling water, cook **Vegetable** until tender-crisp; drain in colander.

3. In same skillet over medium heat, in hot butter, cook salmon patties until browned on both sides. Remove from skillet.

4. In same skillet, combine remaining **Soup,** sour cream and milk, stirring until smooth. Stir in noodles, **Seasoning** and cooked vegetable. Arrange salmon patties over noodle mixture. Cover; cook over low heat 10 minutes or until heated through. Makes 4 servings.

CALORIE AND SODIUM GUIDE (PER SERVING)

Recipe	Calories	Sodium (mg)
Fruited Chops (page 64)		
Row 1 (pork)	649	1494
Row 2 (lamb)	407	1478
Row 3 (smoked pork)	641	3158
Row 4 (veal)	529	1499
Oriental Skillet (page 66)		
Row 1 (turkey)	284	787
Row 2 (chicken)	272	807
Row 3 (veal)	343	862
Meat-Vegetable Packets (page 67)		
Row 1 (golden mushroom)	339	688
Row 2 (cream of chicken)	461	772
Row 3 (Cheddar cheese)	480	770
Row 4 (cream of celery)	351	738
Teriyaki Beef Kabobs (page 69)		
Row 1 (Spanish style vegetable)	360	1140
Row 2 (French onion)	357	1253
Row 3 (beef broth)	327	950
Row 4 (tomato bisque)	385	1224
Vegetable-Stuffed Beef Bundles (page 70)		
Row 1 (green beans)	639	502
Row 2 (zucchini)	662	528
Row 3 (dill pickle spears)	639	571
Beef Stew (page 71)		
Row 1 (salad oil)	591	386
Row 2 (shortening)	630	463
Row 3 (butter)	620	507
Row 4 (bacon drippings)	684	543
Garden Swiss Steak (page 72)		
Row 1 (tomato)	269	613
Row 2 (cream of onion)	289	717
Row 3 (cream of mushroom)	294	689
Row 4 (cream of potato)	274	787
Easy Pot Roast (page 73)		
Row 1 (shortening)	481	460
Row 2 (salad oil)	504	412
Row 3 (non-stick cooking spray)	493	431
Row 4 (bacon drippings)	505	412
Stir-Fried Beef and Vegetables (page 74)		
Row 1 (beef broth)	513	1796
Row 2 (French onion)	569	2029
Row 3 (chicken broth)	617	1529
Row 4 (chicken with rice)	441	1951
Ribs and Lentils (page 76)		
Row 1 (lamb breast)	428	995
Row 2 (beef short ribs)	810	1120
Row 3 (pork spareribs)	662	1056

Recipe	Calories	Sodium (mg)
Brown Rice Supper (page 77)		
Row 1 (chicken)	568	877
Row 2 (pork chops)	385	1004
Row 3 (smoked pork chops)	415	1154
Row 4 (shrimp)	372	982
Baked Chicken Florida (page 79)		
Row 1 (Spanish style vegetable)	123	473
Row 2 (chicken broth)	141	464
Row 3 (chicken with rice)	136	351
Chicken Breasts in Mushroom Sauce (page 80)		
Row 1 (green onions)	205	529
Row 2 (celery)	211	516
Row 3 (carrot)	198	414
Row 4 (leek)	210	507
Crispy Baked Chicken (page 81)		
Row 1 (Cheddar cheese)	476	993
Row 2 (cream of mushroom)	384	1019
Row 3 (cream of chicken)	305	800
Row 4 (creamy chicken mushroom)	400	1015
Chicken Paprika (page 82)		
Row 1 (cream of chicken)	308	716
Row 2 (cream of onion)	302	734
Row 3 (cream of mushroom)	311	691
Row 4 (cream of celery)	302	731
Lemon-Herbed Chicken (page 83)		
Row 1 (cream of chicken)	237	654
Row 2 (cream of celery)	228	667
Row 3 (cream of mushroom)	230	632
Row 4 (creamy chicken mushroom)	241	717
Cornish Hens and Vegetables (page 84)		
Row 1 (mushrooms)	312	762
Row 2 (zucchini)	334	873
Row 3 (tomato)	344	829
Row 4 (celery)	311	628
Sautéed Chicken Livers (page 85)		
Row 1 (onion)	230	775
Row 2 (mushrooms)	251	887
Row 3 (apple)	311	873
Row 4 (green pepper)	241	612
Meatball Stew (page 86)		
Row 1 (soft bread crumbs)	437	846
Row 2 (dry bread crumbs)	508	855
Row 3 (saltines)	469	694
Row 4 (quick-cooking oats)	558	636

CALORIE AND SODIUM GUIDE (PER SERVING)

Recipe	Calories	Sodium (mg)
Savory Meatballs (page 88)		
Row 1 (cream of onion)	433	804
Row 2 (cream of mushroom)	424	761
Row 3 (cream of celery)	413	763
Row 4 (golden mushroom)	411	841
Sausage and Peppers (page 89)		
Row 1 (Spanish style vegetable)	327	1321
Row 2 (tomato bisque)	362	1371
Row 3 (tomato)	331	1242
Tacos (page 90)		
Row 1 (ground beef)	530	832
Row 2 (ground pork)	714	894
Row 3 (cooked beef)	467	801
Row 4 (bulk pork sausage)	570	2634
Best-Ever Meat Loaf (page 92)		
Row 1 (golden mushroom)	446	503
Row 2 (cream of mushroom)	355	499
Row 3 (Cheddar cheese)	518	727
Miniature Meat Loaves (page 93)		
Row 1 (vegetarian vegetable)	291	450
Row 2 (minestrone)	342	644
Row 3 (Spanish style vegetable)	282	382
Souper Enchiladas (page 95)		
Row 1 (black bean)	723	1924
Row 2 (bean with bacon)	898	1755
Row 3 (chili beef)	775	1744
Chimichangas (page 96)		
Row 1 (tomato bisque)	271	459
Row 2 (tomato rice)	269	562
Row 3 (tomato)	255	453
Row 4 (chili beef)	383	485
Tostadas (page 97)		
Row 1 (chicken)	292	653
Row 2 (beef)	290	651
Row 3 (pork)	357	759
Row 4 (ham)	335	807
Rice Pizza (page 98)		
Row 1 (Cheddar)	413	885
Row 2 (mozzarella)	351	690
Row 3 (Monterey Jack)	406	755
Row 4 (colby)	412	852
Quick Stovetop Supper (page 99)		
Row 1 (cream of mushroom)	194	1873
Row 2 (cream of celery)	191	1051
Row 3 (cream of chicken)	195	754
Row 4 (Cheddar cheese)	230	1046

Recipe	Calories	Sodium (mg)
Supper à la King (page 100)		
Row 1 (cream of chicken)	281	606
Row 2 (cream of asparagus)	236	657
Row 3 (cream of mushroom)	279	588
Row 4 (cream of celery)	271	993
Creamy Noodle Supper (page 102)		
Row 1 (cream of chicken)	377	777
Row 2 (cream of shrimp)	388	1182
Row 3 (cream of mushroom)	428	1370
Row 4 (cream of onion)	397	782
Curried Noodle Pie (page 103)		
Row 1 (cream of onion)	343	590
Row 2 (cream of chicken)	503	512
Row 3 (cream of mushroom)	421	528
Row 4 (golden mushroom)	317	908
Stuffed Cabbage Leaves (page 105)		
Row 1 (ground pork)	442	607
Row 2 (ground lamb)	329	567
Row 3 (ground beef)	304	679
Cheesy Rice Bake (page 106)		
Row 1 (cream of mushroom)	307	821
Row 2 (tomato)	290	486
Row 3 (Cheddar cheese)	233	959
Row 4 (cream of onion)	260	571
Chicken-Stuffing Bake (page 107)		
Row 1 (cream of chicken)	457	1289
Row 2 (cream of mushroom)	447	1221
Row 3 (cream of onion)	436	1302
Row 4 (Cheddar cheese)	396	1261
Souper Easy Quiche (page 108)		
Row 1 (Cheddar cheese)	382	892
Row 2 (cream of mushroom)	357	960
Row 3 (cream of onion)	331	756
Row 4 (cream of celery)	332	700
Eggs Goldenrod (page 110)		
Row 1 (cream of celery)	238	859
Row 2 (cream of chicken)	235	1001
Row 3 (cream of onion)	318	1014
Row 4 (cream of mushroom)	306	917
Versatile Crepes (page 111)		
Row 1 (cream of chicken)	448	834
Row 2 (cream of mushroom)	466	1120
Row 3 (Cheddar cheese)	451	1165
Row 4 (cream of onion)	382	793
Easy Soufflé (page 113)		
Row 1 (Cheddar cheese)	222	648
Row 2 (cream of asparagus)	194	590
Row 3 (tomato)	193	708
Row 4 (cream of chicken)	206	628

CALORIE AND SODIUM GUIDE (PER SERVING)

Recipe	Calories	Sodium (mg)
Cheese Omelet Roll (page 114)		
Row 1 (cream of celery)	495	1041
Row 2 (cream of chicken)	348	943
Row 3 (Cheddar cheese)	346	1002
Main Dish Spoonbread (page 115)		
Row 1 (bacon)	284	977
Row 2 (ham)	306	933
Row 3 (bulk pork sausage)	306	1042
Row 4 (corned beef)	517	1507
Vegetable Lasagna (page 116)		
Row 1 (broccoli)	730	1765
Row 2 (spinach)	749	1796
Row 3 (zucchini)	735	1523
Row 4 (green beans)	694	1669
Lasagna Roll-Ups (page 118)		
Row 1 (Italian sausage)	485	795
Row 2 (ground pork)	594	509
Row 3 (ground beef)	640	539
Baked Manicotti (page 119)		
Row 1 (basil leaves)	570	824
Row 2 (oregano leaves)	598	1138
Row 3 (marjoram leaves)	581	1133
Pasta with White Seafood Sauce (page 120)		
Row 1 (parsley)	486	583
Row 2 (basil leaves)	574	684
Row 3 (chives)	540	569
Row 4 (oregano leaves)	554	474

Recipe	Calories	Sodium (mg)
Pasta with Shrimp Sauce (page 121)		
Row 1 (scallops)	628	907
Row 2 (clams)	438	893
Row 3 (cod)	541	871
Row 4 (shrimp)	514	1005
Vegetable-Stuffed Fish Rolls (page 123)		
Row 1 (cream of shrimp)	366	763
Row 2 (cream of mushroom)	223	704
Row 3 (Cheddar cheese)	356	708
Row 4 (cream of celery)	274	713
Fish-Vegetable Bake (page 124)		
Row 1 (spinach)	345	956
Row 2 (broccoli)	349	895
Row 3 (asparagus)	395	869
Perfect Tuna Casserole (page 125)		
Row 1 (cream of mushroom)	267	1000
Row 2 (cream of onion)	289	1283
Row 3 (cream of shrimp)	256	1032
Row 4 (New England clam chowder)	225	1040
Salmon and Noodle Skillet (page 126)		
Row 1 (cream of celery)	466	1138
Row 2 (cream of mushroom)	485	1165
Row 3 (cream of chicken)	509	1193
Row 4 (Cheddar cheese)	532	1221

Accompaniments

✠

Vegetables Oriental

1 can (10½ to 10¾ ounces) condensed **Soup**
2 tablespoons cornstarch
½ teaspoon sugar
¼ teaspoon ground ginger
2 tablespoons dry sherry
1 tablespoon soy sauce
4 cups fresh or frozen **Vegetable 1**
1 cup thinly sliced carrots
Vegetable 2
Garnish

Soup	Vegetable 1	Vegetable 2	Garnish
chicken broth	cut broccoli	2 cups fresh or frozen snow pea pods	diced tofu
French onion	cut asparagus	2 cups fresh bean sprouts	sliced almonds
beef broth	peas	1 can (8 ounces) sliced water chestnuts, drained	sesame seed

1. In 10-inch skillet, combine **Soup,** cornstarch, sugar, ginger, sherry and soy sauce. Over medium heat, heat to boiling, stirring constantly. Add **Vegetable 1** and carrots. Reduce heat to low. Cover; simmer 10 minutes or until vegetables are tender, stirring occasionally.

2. Stir in **Vegetable 2.** Cook until heated through, stirring often. Sprinkle with **Garnish.** Serve with additional soy sauce. Makes about 4 cups, 6 servings.

Tomato Vegetable Skillet

2 tablespoons salad oil
1 large onion, chopped
1 medium green pepper, cut into strips
1 clove garlic, minced
1 can (10½ to 11 ounces) condensed **Soup**
Vegetable
Seasoning
1 tablespoon lemon juice
Cheese

Soup	Vegetable	Seasoning	Cheese
tomato bisque	6 cups sliced zucchini	½ teaspoon basil leaves, crushed	¼ cup grated Parmesan
Spanish style vegetable	6 cups cubed eggplant	½ teaspoon oregano leaves, crushed	½ cup crumbled feta
tomato	4 cups fresh or frozen cut green beans	½ teaspoon thyme leaves, crushed	1 cup shredded Cheddar
tomato rice	4 cups fresh or frozen sliced okra	1 teaspoon chili powder	1 cup shredded Monterey Jack

1. In 10-inch skillet over medium heat, in hot oil, cook onion, green pepper and garlic until tender, stirring occasionally.

2. Stir in **Soup, Vegetable, Seasoning** and lemon juice. Heat to boiling. Reduce heat to low. Cover; simmer 5 to 15 minutes until vegetable is nearly tender, stirring occasionally. Uncover; simmer until sauce is desired consistency.

3. Sprinkle with **Cheese.** Cook 2 minutes more or until cheese is melted. Makes 6 servings.

Honey-Glazed Vegetables

1 can (10½ to 10¾ ounces) condensed **Soup**
¼ cup honey
1 tablespoon cornstarch
1 teaspoon grated orange peel
⅛ teaspoon ground **Spice**
Vegetable
Garnish

Soup	Spice	Vegetable	Garnish
beef broth	cinnamon	2 pounds sweet potatoes, cooked, drained, peeled and cut into lengthwise quarters	slivered orange peel
French onion	nutmeg	2 pounds carrots, sliced, cooked and drained	grated Parmesan cheese
chicken broth	ginger	2 large acorn squash, cooked, drained and cut into ½-inch slices	raisins
chicken gumbo	cardamom	2 pounds parsnips, peeled, sliced, cooked and drained	chopped peanuts

1. In 10-inch skillet, combine **Soup,** honey, cornstarch, grated orange peel and **Spice.** Over medium heat, cook until thickened, stirring constantly.

2. Add **Vegetable.** Over low heat, cook 10 minutes or until vegetable is glazed, basting frequently. Turn into serving bowl; top with **Garnish.** Makes 6 servings.

To Microwave: Cook **Vegetable** according to microwave manufacturer's directions. In 3-quart microwave-safe casserole, combine **Soup,** honey, cornstarch, orange peel and **Spice.** Microwave on HIGH 4 minutes or until boiling and thickened, stirring twice. Add vegetable; cover. Microwave on HIGH 4 to 8 minutes until vegetable is glazed, stirring occasionally. Top with **Garnish.**

Curried Vegetables

1 can (10¾ ounces) condensed **Soup**
⅓ cup milk
½ teaspoon curry powder
4 cups drained, cooked **Vegetable**
Garnish

Soup	Vegetable	Garnish
cream of chicken	cut broccoli	½ cup French-fried onions
cream of celery	cut green beans	2 tablespoons toasted slivered almonds
cream of onion	cauliflowerets	2 tablespoons chopped peanuts

1. In 3-quart saucepan, stir together **Soup,** milk and curry powder until smooth.

2. Stir in **Vegetable.** Over medium heat, heat through, stirring occasionally. Pour into serving dish; sprinkle with **Garnish.** Makes about 4 cups, 6 servings.

To Microwave: In 2-quart microwave-safe casserole, stir together **Soup,** milk and curry powder until smooth. Stir in **Vegetable;** cover. Microwave on HIGH 4 to 6 minutes until heated through, stirring occasionally. Sprinkle with **Garnish.**

Onion-Vegetable Bake

1 can (10¾ to 11 ounces) condensed **Soup**
½ cup **Liquid**
1 teaspoon soy sauce
Dash pepper
4 cups drained, cooked **Vegetable**
1 can (2.8 ounces) French-fried onions

Soup	Liquid	Vegetable
cream of mushroom	milk	cut green beans
cream of celery	light cream	sliced carrots
cream of chicken	plain yogurt	cut broccoli
Cheddar cheese	sour cream	Brussels sprouts

1. In 1½-quart casserole, combine **Soup, Liquid,** soy sauce and pepper. Stir in **Vegetable** and ½ of the onions.

2. Bake at 350°F. 25 minutes or until hot. Top with remaining onions. Bake 5 minutes more. Makes 6 servings.

Tip: *Buy 1 package (16 to 20 ounces) frozen vegetables, 2 packages (9 to 10 ounces each) frozen vegetables, 2 cans (about 16 ounces each) canned vegetables, or about 1½ pounds fresh vegetables for this recipe.*

To Microwave: In 2-quart microwave-safe casserole, combine **Soup, Liquid,** soy sauce and pepper. Stir in **Vegetable** and ½ of the onions; cover. Microwave on HIGH 4 to 7 minutes until hot, stirring once. Top with remaining onions.

Company Cauliflower

1 large head cauliflower (about 1½ pounds), cut into flowerets
2 tablespoons butter or margarine
½ cup chopped green pepper
1 cup sliced mushrooms
1 can (10¾ to 11 ounces) condensed **Soup**
Liquid
Cheese
1 tablespoon chopped pimento
Topping

Soup	Liquid	Cheese	Topping
Cheddar cheese	½ cup chicken broth	1 cup shredded Cheddar	chopped fresh parsley
cream of celery	½ cup milk	1 cup shredded Swiss	toasted sesame seed
cream of mushroom	⅓ cup light cream plus 2 tablespoons dry white wine	½ cup grated Romano	buttered bread crumbs
cream of onion	½ cup water	¼ cup crumbled blue cheese	sliced almonds

1. In covered 10-inch skillet over medium heat, in 1 inch boiling water, cook cauliflower 10 minutes or until tender-crisp. Remove from heat; drain in colander.

2. In same skillet over medium heat, in hot butter, cook green pepper and mushrooms until tender, stirring occasionally. Stir in **Soup** and **Liquid;** mix well. Stir in **Cheese** and pimento.

3. Return cauliflower to skillet; heat through. Sprinkle with **Topping** before serving. Makes about 5 cups, 8 servings.

To Microwave: Use ingredients as above but omit **Liquid.** In 2-quart microwave-safe casserole, combine cauliflower and ¼ cup water; cover. Microwave on HIGH 6 to 8 minutes until tender-crisp, stirring twice. Let stand, covered, 2 to 3 minutes. Drain in colander. In same casserole, combine butter, green pepper and mushrooms; cover. Microwave on HIGH 3 to 5 minutes until green pepper is tender, stirring once. Stir in **Soup, Cheese,** pimento and cauliflower; cover. Microwave on HIGH 5 to 8 minutes until heated through, stirring occasionally. Sprinkle with **Topping.**

Scalloped Vegetables

1 can (10¾ to 11 ounces) condensed **Soup**
½ cup milk
¼ cup chopped fresh parsley
Dash pepper
4 cups **Vegetable 1**
Vegetable 2
1 tablespoon butter or margarine
Garnish

Soup	Vegetable 1	Vegetable 2	Garnish
cream of mushroom	thinly sliced potatoes	1 small onion, thinly sliced	paprika
cream of celery	sliced cauliflower	½ cup thinly sliced celery	pimento strips
cream of onion	fresh or frozen corn kernels	½ cup finely chopped green pepper	cooked, crumbled bacon
Cheddar cheese	thinly sliced turnips	½ cup thinly sliced carrots	shredded Cheddar cheese

1. In small bowl, combine **Soup,** milk, parsley and pepper. In 1½-quart casserole, arrange alternate layers of **Vegetable 1, Vegetable 2** and soup mixture, ending with soup mixture. Dot with butter; cover.

2. Bake at 375°F. 1 hour. Uncover; bake 15 minutes more or until vegetables are tender. Sprinkle with **Garnish.** Makes 6 servings.

To Microwave: Prepare as above in Step 1 but assemble in 2-quart microwave-safe casserole; cover. Microwave on HIGH 18 to 22 minutes until vegetables are tender, rotating dish 2 or 3 times. Sprinkle with **Garnish.**

Vegetable Timbales

4 eggs
1 can (10¾ ounces) condensed **Soup**
1 cup milk
Seasoning
1 cup shredded **Cheese**
¼ cup butter or margarine
3 cups shredded carrots
½ pound mushrooms, chopped
1 package (9 to 10 ounces) frozen **Vegetable,** thawed and drained

Soup	Seasoning	Cheese	Vegetable
cream of onion	¼ teaspoon ground nutmeg	Swiss	chopped spinach
cream of asparagus	½ teaspoon tarragon leaves, crushed	mozzarella	chopped broccoli
cream of mushroom	½ teaspoon dill weed, crushed	Monterey Jack	French-style green beans

1. Generously grease eight 5-ounce custard cups or individual molds.

2. In large bowl, beat eggs until foamy. Stir in **Soup,** milk and **Seasoning;** stir in **Cheese.** Set aside.

3. In 10-inch skillet over medium heat, in hot butter, cook carrots, mushrooms and **Vegetable** until tender and all liquid evaporates, stirring occasionally. Add to soup mixture; stir to mix well.

4. Pour into prepared cups. Place cups in large baking pan on oven rack. Pour boiling water around cups to reach halfway up sides of cups.

5. Bake at 400°F. 30 minutes or until knife inserted in center comes out clean. Let stand 10 minutes; unmold onto serving platter. Makes 8 servings.

Tip: *To make a vegetable casserole, prepare as above in Steps 2 and 3. Pour into greased 2-quart casserole. Bake at 400°F. 45 to 50 minutes until knife inserted in center comes out clean. Let stand 10 minutes before serving.*

Skillet Potatoes

3 tablespoons butter or margarine
1 cup **Vegetable 1**
½ cup **Vegetable 2**
2 cloves garlic, minced
1 can (10¾ ounces) condensed chicken broth
¼ cup water
4 cups cubed potatoes
1 cup carrots cut into julienne strips
Seasoning
Garnish

Vegetable 1	Vegetable 2	Seasoning	Garnish
sliced celery	chopped onion	⅛ teaspoon pepper	chopped fresh parsley
frozen French-style green beans, thawed	sliced green onions with tops	¼ teaspoon thyme leaves, crushed	chopped fresh chives
sliced mushrooms	chopped leeks	⅛ teaspoon dry mustard	toasted sesame seed
chopped tomatoes	chopped green pepper	⅛ teaspoon crushed red pepper	chopped pimento

1. In 10-inch skillet over medium heat, in hot butter, cook **Vegetable 1, Vegetable 2** and garlic until vegetables are tender, stirring occasionally.

2. Add broth, water, potatoes, carrots and **Seasoning** to skillet. Heat to boiling; reduce heat to low. Cover; simmer 15 minutes or until potatoes are tender.

3. Uncover; over medium heat, simmer 5 minutes or until broth is slightly thickened, stirring often. Sprinkle with **Garnish** before serving. Makes about 5 cups, 6 servings.

Vegetable Strudel

1 tablespoon salad oil
½ cup chopped onion
½ cup sliced mushrooms
1 can (10¾ ounces) condensed **Soup**
½ cup shredded **Cheese**
Seasoning
¼ pound phyllo (strudel leaves)
¼ cup butter or margarine, melted
2 cups drained, cooked **Vegetable**
⅓ cup milk
1 tablespoon chopped fresh parsley
½ teaspoon prepared mustard

Soup	Cheese	Seasoning	Vegetable
creamy chicken mushroom	Edam	¼ teaspoon ground nutmeg	cut asparagus
cream of onion	Swiss	1 teaspoon Worcestershire	cut broccoli
cream of mushroom	Cheddar	1 teaspoon chopped fresh chives	diced carrots

1. In small saucepan over medium heat, in hot oil, cook onion and mushrooms until tender, stirring occasionally. Remove from heat; stir in ½ cup of the **Soup, Cheese** and **Seasoning.** Cool slightly.

2. Grease large baking sheet; preheat oven to 375°F. Place 1 phyllo sheet on work surface and brush with melted butter. (While working, cover remaining phyllo with damp towel to prevent drying.) Stack remaining phyllo on buttered sheet, one at a time, brushing each with melted butter.

3. Spread soup mixture on dough, leaving 1 inch border on all sides. Arrange **Vegetable** on top. Fold in 1 inch of short ends of dough; roll up jelly-roll fashion, starting at long side. Carefully lift strudel and place seam side down on prepared baking sheet. Brush with melted butter.

4. Bake 25 minutes or until golden brown. Cool slightly while preparing sauce.

5. In small saucepan, combine remaining **Soup,** milk, parsley and mustard. Over medium heat, heat through, stirring occasionally. Cut strudel into slices and serve with sauce. Makes 6 servings.

Tip: *Place a sheet of waxed paper on work surface before assembling strudel, then use it to help roll up strudel.*

Potato Boats

6 large baking potatoes
2 tablespoons butter or margarine
Seasoning
1 can (11 ounces) condensed Cheddar cheese soup
2 tablespoons **Addition**
Garnish

Seasoning	Addition	Garnish
4 slices bacon, cooked, drained and crumbled	chopped green onions	paprika
½ teaspoon thyme leaves, crushed	chopped fresh parsley	ground nutmeg
⅛ teaspoon cayenne pepper	chopped fresh chives	toasted sesame seed
2 teaspoons prepared mustard	chopped pimento	shredded Cheddar cheese

1. Scrub potatoes; rub lightly with oil. With fork, prick potatoes; place on baking sheet. Bake at 400°F. about 1 hour until potatoes are fork-tender.

2. With knife, cut off tops of potatoes. Scoop out pulp from each, leaving a thin shell. In medium bowl with mixer at medium speed, mash potato pulp with butter and **Seasoning.** Gradually add soup and **Addition;** beat until light and fluffy. Spoon potato mixture into shells. Sprinkle with **Garnish.**

3. Place potatoes on baking sheet. Bake at 450°F. 15 minutes or until hot. Makes 6 servings.

Tip: *These potatoes can be baked and stuffed in advance. Omit the final baking time; cover and refrigerate until needed. Bake stuffed potatoes at 400°F. 30 minutes or until hot.*

To Microwave: Scrub potatoes; prick with fork. In 12 by 8-inch microwave-safe dish, arrange potatoes. Microwave on HIGH 20 to 25 minutes until potatoes are almost done, turning over and rearranging potatoes once. Let stand, covered, 5 to 10 minutes. Proceed as in Step 2. Place stuffed shells in same dish. Microwave on HIGH 7 to 10 minutes until hot, rearranging potatoes once.

Broccoli and Noodles Parmesan

1 bunch broccoli (about 1½ pounds)
2 tablespoons butter or margarine
½ cup chopped onion
1 clove garlic, minced
1 can (10¾ to 11 ounces) condensed **Soup**
Seasoning
1 cup shredded **Cheese**
½ cup grated Parmesan cheese
1 cup **Dairy**
8 ounces (about 6 cups) noodles, cooked and drained

Soup	Seasoning	Cheese	Dairy
cream of mushroom	½ teaspoon tarragon leaves, crushed	American	sour cream
cream of onion	½ teaspoon basil leaves, crushed	Cheddar	plain yogurt
cream of chicken	½ teaspoon curry powder	Swiss	ricotta cheese
Cheddar cheese	¼ teaspoon cayenne pepper	Monterey Jack	creamed small curd cottage cheese

1. Cut broccoli into bite-sized pieces. In covered 4-quart saucepan over medium heat, in 1 inch boiling water, cook broccoli 6 minutes or until tender. Drain in colander.

2. In same saucepan over medium heat, in hot butter, cook onion and garlic until tender, stirring occasionally. Stir in **Soup** and **Seasoning;** mix well.

3. Add **Cheese** and Parmesan, stirring until melted. Stir in **Dairy,** broccoli and cooked noodles. Pour into 2-quart casserole. Cover; bake at 350°F. 30 minutes or until bubbly. Makes 8 servings.

Tip: *To make clean-up easy, cook noodles first in 4-quart saucepan, then use it to cook broccoli, then sauce. Add broccoli to same colander with noodles to drain.*

To Microwave: Cut broccoli into bite-sized pieces. In 3-quart microwave-safe casserole, combine broccoli and ½ cup water; cover. Microwave on HIGH 6 to 8 minutes until almost tender. Let stand, covered, 2 to 3 minutes. Drain in colander. In same casserole, combine butter, onion and garlic; cover. Microwave on HIGH 2 to 2½ minutes until onion is tender. Stir in **Soup, Seasoning, Cheese** and Parmesan. Stir in **Dairy,** broccoli and cooked noodles; cover. Microwave on HIGH 8 to 10 minutes until heated through, stirring occasionally. Let stand, covered, 2 to 3 minutes.

Stuffed Vegetables

Vegetable
3 slices bacon, diced
1½ cups chopped mushrooms
½ cup chopped green onions
1 can (10¾ to 11 ounces) condensed **Soup**
1 cup fresh or frozen whole kernel corn
Cheese
¼ cup milk
¼ teaspoon **Herb,** crushed
Paprika

Vegetable	Soup	Cheese	Herb
3 zucchini, halved lengthwise	cream of mushroom	½ cup shredded Swiss	tarragon leaves
3 green peppers, halved lengthwise	cream of celery	¼ cup grated Parmesan	summer savory leaves
6 medium tomatoes with ½-inch slice removed from top	Cheddar cheese	½ cup shredded sharp Cheddar	basil leaves

1. Remove seeds and pulp, if any, from **Vegetable,** leaving ¼-inch shell. In 10-inch skillet over medium heat, in 1 inch boiling water, cook zucchini shells or peppers 2 minutes. (Do not cook tomatoes; invert tomato shells on paper towels to drain.) Drain well. Discard water.

2. In same skillet over medium heat, cook bacon until crisp. Remove with slotted spoon; drain on paper towels. In bacon drippings, cook mushrooms and green onions until tender, stirring occasionally. Remove from heat. Stir in ½ cup of the **Soup,** corn, **Cheese** and reserved bacon.

3. In 12 by 8-inch baking dish, arrange vegetable shells. Spoon corn mixture into shells. Bake at 350°F. 20 minutes or until hot.

4. Meanwhile, in small saucepan, combine remaining **Soup,** milk and **Herb.** Over low heat, heat just until hot, stirring occasionally. Spoon sauce over stuffed vegetables; sprinkle with paprika. Makes 6 servings.

Cheesy Noodles

8 ounces (about 6 cups) wide noodles
¼ cup butter or margarine
1 can (10¾ to 11 ounces) condensed **Soup**
Liquid
Cheese
Garnish

Soup	Liquid	Cheese	Garnish
cream of mushroom	¾ cup milk	½ cup grated Parmesan	grated Parmesan cheese
cream of onion	¾ cup evaporated milk	½ cup grated Romano	poppy seed
Cheddar cheese	¾ cup light cream	½ cup grated Gruyère	chopped fresh parsley
creamy chicken mushroom	¾ cup sour cream plus ¼ cup milk	1 cup shredded Cheddar	sliced pitted ripe olives

1. In 4-quart saucepan over high heat, in large amount boiling water, cook noodles 7 to 9 minutes until tender. Drain; return to saucepan and toss with butter.

2. Meanwhile, in medium bowl, stir together **Soup, Liquid** and **Cheese.** Stir into buttered noodles. Over medium heat, heat through, stirring constantly. Turn into serving dish; sprinkle with **Garnish.** Makes about 5 cups, 8 servings.

Macaroni and Cheese

1 can (10¾ to 11 ounces) condensed **Soup**
¾ cup **Liquid**
1 teaspoon prepared mustard
⅛ teaspoon pepper
6 ounces (about 1½ cups) elbow macaroni, cooked and drained
2 cups shredded **Cheese**
Topper

Soup	Liquid	Cheese	Topper
cream of mushroom	milk	Cheddar	1 cup French-fried onions
cream of onion	water	American	1 cup coarsely crushed potato chips
cream of celery	evaporated milk	Swiss	¼ cup buttered bread crumbs
Cheddar cheese	tomato juice	Monterey Jack	1 medium tomato, sliced

1. In 1½-quart casserole, stir together **Soup, Liquid,** mustard and pepper. Stir in macaroni and 1½ cups of the **Cheese.** Bake at 400°F. 25 minutes or until hot; stir.

2. Sprinkle with remaining ½ cup **Cheese** and **Topper;** bake 5 minutes more or until cheese melts. Makes 6 servings.

Tip: *To make buttered crumbs, toss ¼ cup fine dry bread crumbs with 1 tablespoon butter or margarine, melted.*

To Microwave: In 2-quart microwave-safe casserole, stir together **Soup, Liquid,** mustard, pepper, macaroni and 1½ cups of the **Cheese;** cover. Microwave on HIGH 7 to 10 minutes until hot, stirring occasionally. Sprinkle with remaining ½ cup **Cheese** and **Topper.** Microwave, uncovered, on HIGH 30 to 45 seconds until cheese melts.

Gnocchi

1 cup milk
½ cup butter or margarine
1 cup all-purpose flour
3 eggs
1 can (10¾ to 11 ounces) condensed **Soup**
Liquid
½ cup shredded **Cheese**
¼ cup grated Parmesan cheese
Garnish

Soup	Liquid	Cheese	Garnish
cream of onion	1 cup light cream	Swiss	paprika
cream of celery	½ cup dry white wine plus ½ cup milk	Gruyère	nutmeg
cream of chicken	1 cup evaporated milk	American	toasted sesame seed
Cheddar cheese	½ cup beer plus ½ cup water	sharp Cheddar	chopped fresh parsley

1. In 2-quart saucepan over medium heat, heat milk and butter until mixture boils. Reduce heat to low. With wooden spoon, stir in flour all at once. Stir until mixture leaves sides of pan. Remove from heat. Stir in eggs, one at a time, beating well after each addition. Cover; cool dough slightly.

2. In 2-quart saucepan over high heat, heat 3 cups water to boiling; reduce heat to low. Spoon dough into decorating bag with ¾-inch round tip. Holding bag over simmering water, squeeze dough into 1-inch lengths; with knife, cut dough so it drops into water. Repeat, cooking about ⅓ of the dough at a time. Cook 3 minutes or until pieces float to surface. Remove gnocchi with slotted spoon to 12 by 8-inch baking dish.

3. In 2-quart saucepan over medium heat, heat **Soup** and **Liquid,** stirring constantly. Stir in **Cheese;** heat through. Pour sauce over gnocchi. Sprinkle with Parmesan cheese and **Garnish.**

4. Bake at 350°F. 30 minutes or until bubbly. Makes 6 servings.

Tip: *If you don't have a decorating bag for shaping gnocchi, simply drop dough by rounded teaspoonfuls into simmering water. Proceed as above.*

Savory Pilaf

2 tablespoons butter or margarine
1 cup **Vegetable**
½ cup sliced green onions
1 clove garlic, minced
1 cup **Grain**
1 can (10½ to 10¾ ounces) condensed **Soup**
¾ cup water
Seasoning
2 tablespoons chopped fresh parsley

Vegetable	Grain	Soup	Seasoning
shredded carrots	raw regular rice	chicken gumbo	¼ teaspoon marjoram leaves, crushed
chopped green or red pepper	raw brown rice	French onion	¼ teaspoon curry powder
chopped tomato	raw pearled barley	beef broth	¼ teaspoon oregano leaves, crushed
chopped celery	raw bulgur wheat	chicken broth	½ teaspoon rubbed sage

1. In 3-quart saucepan over medium heat, in hot butter, cook **Vegetable,** green onions and garlic until tender, stirring occasionally. Stir in **Grain;** cook 5 minutes more, stirring occasionally.

2. Stir in **Soup,** water and **Seasoning.** Heat to boiling. Reduce heat to low; cover. Simmer until grain is tender (about 25 minutes for regular rice, 50 minutes for brown rice, 1 hour for barley, 15 minutes for bulgur); stir occasionally. Add more water during cooking if mixture appears dry. Garnish with parsley. Makes about 3 cups, 4 servings.

Vegetable Pancakes

1 can (10¾ ounces) condensed **Soup**
4 cups shredded **Vegetable**
½ cup finely chopped onion
1 egg, beaten
¼ cup all-purpose flour
2 tablespoons salad oil
½ cup sour cream
Seasoning

Soup	Vegetable	Seasoning
cream of mushroom	zucchini	¼ teaspoon curry powder
cream of celery	peeled sweet potatoes	¼ teaspoon ground nutmeg
cream of onion	peeled potatoes	2 tablespoons chopped fresh chives

1. In large bowl, combine ⅓ cup of the **Soup, Vegetable,** onion, egg and flour; stir to combine. Let stand 15 minutes.

2. In 10-inch skillet over medium-low heat, heat oil. Drop vegetable mixture by rounded tablespoons into skillet, making 4 pancakes at a time; press with spoon to flatten to 2½-inch rounds. Fry until golden brown, turning once. Drain on paper towels; keep warm. Repeat with remaining vegetable mixture, adding more oil to skillet if needed.

3. In small saucepan, stir together remaining **Soup,** sour cream and **Seasoning** until smooth; over medium heat, heat through, stirring occasionally. Serve pancakes with sauce. Makes 6 servings.

Spanish Rice

Meat
½ cup chopped onion
Vegetable
1 clove garlic, minced
1⅓ cups raw regular rice
1 can (10½ to 10¾ ounces) condensed **Soup**
1 cup salsa
1 cup water

Meat	Vegetable	Soup
5 slices bacon, diced	½ cup chopped green pepper	Spanish style vegetable
5 pork sausage links, sliced	½ cup chopped celery and celery leaves	tomato bisque
½ cup diced cooked ham plus 2 tablespoons salad oil	1 can (4 ounces) chopped green chilies, drained	tomato
5 frankfurters, sliced, plus 2 tablespoons salad oil	½ cup chopped carrot	tomato rice

1. In 10-inch skillet over medium heat, cook **Meat** until lightly browned. Stir in onion, **Vegetable** and garlic; cook until vegetables are tender, stirring occasionally.

2. Stir in rice; cook until rice is slightly browned, stirring often. Remove from heat. Stir in **Soup,** salsa and water; mix well. Pour into 2-quart casserole.

3. Cover; bake at 350°F. 40 minutes or until rice is tender. Makes 6 servings.

Mushroom Stuffing

½ cup butter or margarine
1 cup chopped celery
1 cup chopped onion
1 cup sliced mushrooms
1 can (10¾ ounces) condensed **Soup**
½ cup **Liquid**
Bread
¼ cup chopped fresh parsley
Seasoning

Soup	Liquid	Bread	Seasoning
cream of mushroom	milk	1 loaf (16 ounces) white bread, cubed	2 teaspoons rubbed sage
cream of chicken	water	8 cups coarsely crumbled corn bread	1 teaspoon thyme leaves, crushed
cream of celery	apple juice	1 loaf (16 ounces) raisin bread, cubed	1 teaspoon curry powder
creamy chicken mushroom	chicken broth	1 loaf (16 ounces) whole wheat bread, cubed	1 teaspoon tarragon leaves, crushed

1. Grease 2-quart casserole.

2. In 10-inch skillet over medium heat, in hot butter, cook celery, onion and mushrooms until vegetables are tender, stirring often. Remove from heat. Stir in **Soup** and **Liquid;** mix well.

3. In large bowl, combine **Bread,** parsley and **Seasoning.** Pour vegetable mixture over bread; toss to mix well. Turn into prepared casserole.

4. Bake at 350°F. 45 minutes or until golden. Makes 8 servings.

CALORIE AND SODIUM GUIDE (PER SERVING)

Recipe	Calories	Sodium (mg)
Vegetables Oriental (page 130)		
Row 1 (chicken broth)	111	547
Row 2 (French onion)	92	711
Row 3 (beef broth)	136	658
Tomato Vegetable Skillet (page 132)		
Row 1 (tomato bisque)	157	510
Row 2 (Spanish style vegetable)	150	495
Row 3 (tomato)	194	481
Row 4 (tomato rice)	230	506
Honey-Glazed Vegetables (page 133)		
Row 1 (beef broth)	308	372
Row 2 (French onion)	124	526
Row 3 (chicken broth)	145	403
Row 4 (chicken gumbo)	171	463
Curried Vegetables (page 134)		
Row 1 (cream of chicken)	122	519
Row 2 (cream of celery)	100	440
Row 3 (cream of onion)	94	463
Onion-Vegetable Bake (page 135)		
Row 1 (cream of mushroom)	119	520
Row 2 (cream of celery)	153	571
Row 3 (cream of chicken)	129	541
Row 4 (Cheddar cheese)	179	565
Company Cauliflower (page 137)		
Row 1 (Cheddar cheese)	161	525
Row 2 (cream of celery)	150	410
Row 3 (cream of mushroom)	139	448
Row 4 (cream of onion)	105	442
Scalloped Vegetables (page 138)		
Row 1 (cream of mushroom)	151	453
Row 2 (cream of celery)	99	495
Row 3 (cream of onion)	175	485
Row 4 (Cheddar cheese)	126	538
Vegetable Timbales (page 139)		
Row 1 (cream of onion)	258	540
Row 2 (cream of asparagus)	240	562
Row 3 (cream of mushroom)	260	546
Skillet Potatoes (page 140)		
Row 1 (celery)	148	494
Row 2 (green beans)	147	469
Row 3 (mushrooms)	146	471
Row 4 (tomatoes)	143	420
Vegetable Strudel (page 142)		
Row 1 (chicken mushroom)	255	737
Row 2 (cream of onion)	257	659
Row 3 (cream of mushroom)	260	785

Recipe	Calories	Sodium (mg)
Potato Boats (page 143)		
Row 1 (bacon)	274	544
Row 2 (thyme leaves)	245	501
Row 3 (cayenne pepper)	245	493
Row 4 (mustard)	247	516
Broccoli and Noodles Parmesan (page 145)		
Row 1 (cream of mushroom)	342	858
Row 2 (cream of onion)	299	740
Row 3 (cream of chicken)	335	713
Row 4 (Cheddar cheese)	316	850
Stuffed Vegetables (page 146)		
Row 1 (zucchini)	170	494
Row 2 (green peppers)	144	564
Row 3 (tomatoes)	192	569
Cheesy Noodles (page 147)		
Row 1 (cream of mushroom)	300	641
Row 2 (cream of onion)	330	781
Row 3 (Cheddar cheese)	364	585
Row 4 (chicken mushroom)	401	697
Macaroni and Cheese (page 148)		
Row 1 (cream of mushroom)	354	815
Row 2 (cream of onion)	322	995
Row 3 (cream of celery)	326	606
Row 4 (Cheddar cheese)	276	700
Gnocchi (page 149)		
Row 1 (cream of onion)	449	769
Row 2 (cream of celery)	403	763
Row 3 (cream of chicken)	432	892
Row 4 (Cheddar cheese)	410	796
Savory Pilaf (page 150)		
Row 1 (carrots)	302	752
Row 2 (green pepper)	286	780
Row 3 (tomato)	249	681
Row 4 (celery)	235	700
Vegetable Pancakes (page 152)		
Row 1 (cream of mushroom)	162	433
Row 2 (cream of celery)	352	499
Row 3 (cream of onion)	193	499
Spanish Rice (page 153)		
Row 1 (bacon)	256	1395
Row 2 (pork sausage)	309	1606
Row 3 (ham)	304	1514
Row 4 (frankfurters)	395	1955
Mushroom Stuffing (page 154)		
Row 1 (cream of mushroom)	296	705
Row 2 (cream of chicken)	262	731
Row 3 (cream of celery)	307	650
Row 4 (chicken mushroom)	264	777

Salads and Dressings

Garden Pasta Salad

¼ cup salad oil
1 cup sliced mushrooms
½ cup chopped onion
1 clove garlic, minced
1 cup **Vegetable 1**
Vegetable 2
1 teaspoon basil leaves, crushed
4 ounces **Macaroni,** cooked and drained
¼ cup sliced pitted ripe olives
1 can (10½ ounces) condensed Spanish style vegetable soup
¼ cup red wine vinegar
Cheese

Vegetable 1	Vegetable 2	Macaroni	Cheese
thinly sliced zucchini	1 cup broccoli cut into bite-sized pieces	corkscrews	1 cup cubed Muenster
fresh or frozen cut green beans	1 can (8 ounces) red kidney beans, drained	sea shells	1 cup cubed Provolone
fresh or frozen cut asparagus	1 cup diagonally sliced carrots	elbows	¼ cup crumbled blue cheese
fresh or frozen snow pea pods	1 cup cauliflower cut into bite-sized pieces	wagon wheels	⅓ cup grated Parmesan

1. In 10-inch skillet over medium heat, in hot oil, cook mushrooms, onion and garlic about 5 minutes until tender, stirring occasionally.

2. Stir in **Vegetable 1, Vegetable 2** and basil. Cover; cook 5 minutes or until vegetables are tender-crisp, stirring occasionally. Remove from heat.

3. In large bowl, toss together vegetable mixture, cooked **Macaroni,** olives, soup and vinegar. Cover; refrigerate until serving time, at least 4 hours. Just before serving, add **Cheese;** toss lightly. Makes about 5 cups, 6 servings.

Rice Salad

1 can (10¾ ounces) condensed chicken broth
¾ cup water
1 cup raw regular rice
½ cup mayonnaise
½ cup sour cream
Liquid
1 cup chopped celery
Addition 1
Addition 2

Liquid	Addition 1	Addition 2
½ cup pineapple juice	1⅓ cups halved seedless grapes	2 medium bananas, sliced
⅓ cup orange juice plus 3 tablespoons lemon juice	½ cup sliced green onions	2 hard-cooked eggs, chopped
⅓ cup apple juice plus 2 tablespoons vinegar	½ cup green pepper strips	1½ cups halved cherry tomatoes

1. In 2-quart saucepan over high heat, heat broth and water to boiling. Stir in rice. Reduce heat to low. Cover; simmer 20 minutes or until tender. Remove from heat.

2. In large bowl, combine mayonnaise, sour cream and **Liquid;** mix until blended. Stir in rice, celery and **Addition 1.** Cover; refrigerate until serving time, at least 4 hours.

3. Just before serving, stir in **Addition 2.** Makes about 5 cups, 6 servings.

Potato Salad

3 pounds potatoes
1 can (10¾ ounces) condensed **Soup**
¾ cup mayonnaise
2 tablespoons red wine vinegar
Seasoning
1 cup chopped celery
Vegetable 1
½ cup **Vegetable 2**
2 hard-cooked eggs, chopped

Soup	Seasoning	Vegetable 1	Vegetable 2
cream of celery	⅛ teaspoon pepper	¾ cup drained, cooked peas	sliced radishes
cream of chicken	¼ teaspoon dry mustard	¼ cup chopped green onions	chopped cucumber
cream of onion	½ teaspoon celery seed	½ cup drained, cooked diced carrot	chopped green pepper
cream of mushroom	⅛ teaspoon cayenne pepper	½ cup diced zucchini	sliced pitted ripe olives

1. In 4-quart saucepan, place potatoes; add water to cover. Over high heat, heat to boiling. Reduce heat to low; cover. Simmer 20 to 30 minutes until fork-tender; drain. Cool slightly. Peel potatoes; cut potatoes into ½-inch cubes.

2. In large bowl, mix together **Soup,** mayonnaise, vinegar and **Seasoning** until well blended.

3. Add potatoes, celery, **Vegetable 1, Vegetable 2** and eggs; toss gently to mix. Cover; refrigerate until serving time, at least 4 hours. Makes about 7 cups, 8 servings.

German-Style Potato Salad

2 pounds potatoes
2 hard-cooked eggs, sliced
Seasoning
Meat
½ cup chopped onion
2 tablespoons all-purpose flour
2 tablespoons sugar
⅓ cup cider vinegar
1 can (10¾ ounces) condensed chicken broth
⅓ cup water
Dash pepper
Garnish

Seasoning	Meat	Garnish
2 tablespoons chopped parsley	6 slices bacon, diced	chopped green onions
¼ cup shredded carrot	½ cup diced cooked ham plus 2 tablespoons salad oil	chopped green pepper
½ teaspoon celery seed	4 frankfurters, sliced, plus 2 tablespoons salad oil	diced pimento
½ teaspoon dill weed, crushed	½ pound kielbasa, diced, plus 2 tablespoons salad oil	sliced pimento-stuffed olives

1. In 4-quart saucepan, place potatoes; add water to cover. Over high heat, heat to boiling. Reduce heat to low; cover. Simmer 20 to 30 minutes until fork-tender; drain. Cool slightly. Peel potatoes; cut potatoes into slices.

2. In large bowl, combine potatoes, eggs and **Seasoning;** set aside.

3. In 10-inch skillet over medium heat, cook **Meat** and onion until meat is well browned, stirring occasionally. Remove meat and onion with slotted spoon; add to potato mixture. Reserve drippings in skillet.

4. Stir flour into drippings. Cook 1 minute, stirring constantly. Add sugar, vinegar, broth, water and pepper. Cook until mixture boils, stirring constantly. Pour over potato mixture; toss gently to mix well. Sprinkle with **Garnish.** Serve warm. Makes about 6 cups, 8 servings.

Marinated Garden Salad

1 can (10¾ ounces) condensed chicken broth
⅓ cup red wine vinegar
Herb
¼ teaspoon pepper
Vegetable 1
Vegetable 2
1 medium green pepper, cut into strips
1 medium onion, sliced

Herb	Vegetable 1	Vegetable 2
½ teaspoon basil leaves, crushed	3 medium zucchini, thinly sliced	2 medium tomatoes, cut into wedges
2 tablespoons chopped fresh chives	2 medium cucumbers, thinly sliced	2 cups carrots cut into julienne strips
½ teaspoon tarragon leaves, crushed	½ pound snow pea pods	1 can (7 ounces) sliced water chestnuts, drained
½ teaspoon rubbed sage	½ pound small whole mushrooms	2 cups drained, cooked cut green beans

1. In large bowl, combine chicken broth, vinegar, **Herb** and pepper; mix well.

2. Add **Vegetable 1, Vegetable 2,** green pepper and onion; toss gently to mix. Cover; refrigerate until serving time, at least 4 hours, stirring occasionally. Makes about 4 cups, 6 servings.

Blue Ribbon Carrot Salad

2 pounds carrots, cut into 2 by ¼-inch sticks
1 can (10¾ ounces) condensed tomato soup
¼ cup sugar
½ cup vinegar
¼ cup salad oil
1 teaspoon **Seasoning**
1 teaspoon Worcestershire
Vegetable 1
Vegetable 2

Seasoning	Vegetable 1	Vegetable 2
prepared mustard	1 cup sliced celery	1 cup fresh snow pea pods, halved crosswise, cooked and drained
dry mustard	1 medium onion, sliced	1 green pepper, cut into strips
prepared horseradish	½ cup sliced radishes	1 cup drained, cooked cut green beans
chili powder	½ cup sliced green onions	1 medium cucumber, halved lengthwise and sliced

1. In 4-quart saucepan over medium heat, in 1 inch boiling water, cook carrots until tender. Drain; cool slightly.

2. In large bowl, combine soup, sugar, vinegar, oil, **Seasoning** and Worcestershire.

3. Add cooked carrots, **Vegetable 1** and **Vegetable 2;** toss to coat well. Cover; refrigerate until serving time, at least 4 hours. Makes about 6 cups, 8 servings.

To Microwave: In 2-quart microwave-safe casserole, combine carrots and ¼ cup water; cover. Microwave on HIGH 8 to 12 minutes until tender, stirring twice. Let stand, covered, 2 minutes. Drain; cool slightly. Proceed as in Steps 2 and 3.

Crunchy Cucumber Salad

1 can (10¾ ounces) condensed **Soup**
½ cup **Base**
Vegetable 1
Vegetable 2
2 tablespoons wine vinegar
1 tablespoon chopped fresh parsley
4 cups thinly sliced cucumbers
Lettuce

Soup	Base	Vegetable 1	Vegetable 2
cream of celery	sour cream	1 cup sliced celery	1 cup sliced red onion
cream of chicken	plain yogurt	2 cups sweet red pepper strips	¼ cup finely chopped onion
cream of onion	mayonnaise	2 cups shredded carrots	¼ cup chopped green onions

1. In large bowl, combine **Soup, Base, Vegetable 1, Vegetable 2,** vinegar and parsley; stir well. Add cucumbers; stir to mix.

2. Cover; refrigerate until serving time, at least 4 hours. Spoon into lettuce-lined serving bowl. Makes about 4 cups, 8 servings.

Tip: *To make extra-fancy sliced cucumbers, pull a fork lengthwise through skin on all sides before slicing.*

Marinated Bean Relish

1 can (10½ to 10¾ ounces) condensed **Soup**
¼ cup cider vinegar
1 can (15 to 20 ounces) **Beans,** drained
1 medium cucumber, peeled and sliced
1 small onion, sliced
½ cup **Vegetable 1**
Vegetable 2

Soup	Beans	Vegetable 1	Vegetable 2
Spanish style vegetable	garbanzo beans	green pepper strips	1 medium tomato, chopped
tomato	lima beans	carrot cut into julienne strips	1 cup drained, cooked cut green beans
vegetarian vegetable	kidney beans	sliced celery	1 cup canned whole kernel corn, drained

1. In medium bowl, combine **Soup** and vinegar; stir well.

2. Add remaining ingredients; toss to coat well. Cover; refrigerate until serving time, at least 4 hours. Makes about 4 cups, 8 servings.

Creamy Coleslaw

1 can (10½ to 10¾ ounces) condensed **Soup**
½ cup mayonnaise
¼ cup vinegar
½ teaspoon **Seasoning**
8 cups shredded cabbage
Vegetable
¼ cup finely chopped onion

Soup	Seasoning	Vegetable
cream of celery	caraway seed	½ cup chopped green pepper
cream of chicken	tarragon leaves, crushed	½ cup shredded carrot
cream of onion	celery seed	2 tablespoons chopped pimento

1. In large bowl, combine **Soup,** mayonnaise, vinegar and **Seasoning;** stir until smooth.

2. Add remaining ingredients; toss gently to mix well. Cover; refrigerate until serving time, at least 4 hours. Makes about 6 cups, 8 servings.

Fruited Salad Mold

Fruit
2 tablespoons sugar
2 envelopes unflavored gelatin
1 can (10¾ ounces) condensed cream of celery soup
1 container (8 ounces) creamed cottage cheese
Dairy
½ cup **Addition**

Fruit	Dairy	Addition
1 can (20 ounces) crushed pineapple	1 cup heavy cream, whipped	chopped walnuts
2 packages (10 ounces each) frozen raspberries, thawed	1½ cups sour cream	chopped celery
1 can (16 ounces) sliced peaches, cut up	1½ cups plain yogurt	chopped apple
1 can (16 ounces) sliced pears, cut up	1 carton (8 ounces) frozen whipped dessert topping, thawed	shredded carrot

1. Drain **Fruit,** reserving liquid. Measure liquid; add enough water to make 1 cup liquid, if necessary. Pour liquid into 1-quart saucepan; add sugar. Sprinkle gelatin over liquid. Let stand 5 minutes. Over low heat, heat until gelatin is dissolved, stirring constantly. Pour into large bowl.

2. Stir in drained fruit and soup. Refrigerate 1 to 1½ hours until almost set.

3. Fold in cottage cheese, **Dairy** and **Addition.** Pour into 7-cup mold. Refrigerate until set, at least 4 hours or overnight.

4. Unmold onto serving platter. Makes 8 servings.

Buffet Layered Salad

1 can (10¾ ounces) condensed **Soup**
1 cup **Base**
¼ cup grated Parmesan cheese
1 tablespoon grated onion
6 cups torn salad greens
2 medium **Vegetables,** thinly sliced
2 cups sliced mushrooms
2 medium tomatoes, diced
½ cup chopped green onions
Garnish

Soup	Base	Vegetables	Garnish
cream of mushroom	sour cream	carrots	sliced pitted ripe olives
cream of celery	plain yogurt	zucchini	chopped fresh parsley
cream of chicken	mayonnaise	cucumbers	chopped hard-cooked egg

1. For dressing, in medium bowl, combine **Soup, Base,** cheese and onion. Mix until smooth; set aside.

2. In clear 4-quart bowl, layer salad greens, **Vegetables,** mushrooms and tomatoes. Spoon dressing over salad, spreading to cover salad. Cover; refrigerate until serving time, at least 4 hours.

3. Sprinkle with green onions and **Garnish** before serving. Makes 12 servings.

Tip: *Use your favorite salad greens; choose from iceberg, Boston, Bibb and leaf lettuce, as well as spinach, arugula, radicchio and watercress.*

Tomato French Dressing

1 can (10¾ ounces) condensed tomato soup
½ cup salad oil
¼ cup **Liquid**
Seasoning
Flavoring

Liquid	Seasoning	Flavoring
cider vinegar	½ teaspoon dry mustard	4 slices bacon, cooked, drained and crumbled
lemon juice	1 tablespoon grated onion	¼ cup crumbled blue cheese
wine vinegar	1 tablespoon finely chopped green onion	1 clove garlic, minced

1. In covered jar or shaker, combine all ingredients; shake well before using.

2. Serve over mixed salad greens or fruit salads. Makes about 2 cups.

Tomato-Cucumber Dressing

1 can (10¾ ounces) condensed **Soup**
1 cup **Base**
1 cup chopped tomato, drained
½ cup chopped seeded cucumber
Herb
1 tablespoon grated onion
⅛ teaspoon pepper
½ cup milk

Soup	Base	Herb
cream of shrimp	plain yogurt	¼ cup chopped fresh parsley
cream of celery	mayonnaise	2 tablespoons chopped fresh chives
cream of chicken	sour cream	2 tablespoons chopped fresh basil leaves

1. In medium bowl, combine **Soup** and **Base,** stirring until well blended. Add remaining ingredients; mix well. Refrigerate until serving time, at least 4 hours.

2. Serve over mixed salad greens. Makes about 3 cups.

Tip: *This dressing also makes a flavorful dip for crackers or vegetables.*

Creamy Salad Dressing

1 can (10¾ to 11 ounces) condensed **Soup**
½ cup mayonnaise
⅓ cup chopped fresh parsley
Liquid
Seasoning
Flavoring
⅛ teaspoon pepper

Soup	Liquid	Seasoning	Flavoring
cream of asparagus	¼ cup tarragon vinegar	3 green onions, thinly sliced	2 tablespoons finely chopped anchovies
cream of onion	1 tablespoon tomato paste	3 tablespoons sweet pickle relish	1 hard-cooked egg, chopped
cream of mushroom	3 to 4 tablespoons lemon juice	⅓ cup grated Parmesan cheese	2 cloves garlic, minced
Cheddar cheese	¼ cup buttermilk	2 slices bacon, cooked, drained and crumbled	1 tablespoon Worcestershire

1. In small bowl, combine **Soup** and mayonnaise; mix until smooth.

2. Add remaining ingredients; mix well. Cover; refrigerate until serving time, at least 4 hours.

3. Serve over mixed salad greens. Makes about 2 cups.

CALORIE AND SODIUM GUIDE (PER SERVING)

Recipe	Calories	Sodium (mg)
Garden Pasta Salad (page 156)		
Row 1 (zucchini)	247	516
Row 2 (green beans)	269	562
Row 3 (asparagus)	197	481
Row 4 (snow pea pods)	207	478
Rice Salad (page 158)		
Row 1 (pineapple juice)	270	584
Row 2 (orange juice plus lemon juice)	249	607
Row 3 (apple juice plus vinegar)	228	586
Potato Salad (page 159)		
Row 1 (cream of celery)	220	502
Row 2 (cream of chicken)	216	501
Row 3 (cream of onion)	214	527
Row 4 (cream of mushroom)	222	532
German-Style Potato Salad (page 160)		
Row 1 (parsley)	173	405
Row 2 (carrot)	146	251
Row 3 (celery seed)	213	550
Row 4 (dill weed)	226	537
Marinated Garden Salad (page 161)		
Row 1 (basil leaves)	45	406
Row 2 (chives)	43	424
Row 3 (tarragon leaves)	61	413
Row 4 (rubbed sage)	41	411
Blue Ribbon Carrot Salad (page 162)		
Row 1 (prepared mustard)	182	354
Row 2 (dry mustard)	174	298
Row 3 (horseradish)	171	330
Row 4 (chili powder)	173	332
Crunchy Cucumber Salad (page 164)		
Row 1 (cream of celery)	87	355
Row 2 (cream of chicken)	69	334
Row 3 (cream of onion)	118	429

Recipe	Calories	Sodium (mg)
Marinated Bean Relish (page 165)		
Row 1 (Spanish style vegetable)	78	226
Row 2 (tomato)	73	356
Row 3 (vegetarian vegetable)	89	345
Creamy Coleslaw (page 166)		
Row 1 (cream of celery)	114	444
Row 2 (cream of chicken)	119	440
Row 3 (cream of onion)	109	387
Fruited Salad Mold (page 167)		
Row 1 (pineapple)	219	439
Row 2 (raspberries)	246	465
Row 3 (peaches)	151	460
Row 4 (pears)	209	449
Buffet Layered Salad (page 169)		
Row 1 (cream of mushroom)	90	256
Row 2 (cream of celery)	61	261
Row 3 (cream of chicken)	126	388
Tomato French Dressing (page 170)*		
Row 1 (cider vinegar)	44	76
Row 2 (lemon juice)	42	82
Row 3 (wine vinegar)	38	67
Tomato-Cucumber Dressing (page 171)*		
Row 1 (cream of shrimp)	10	59
Row 2 (cream of celery)	27	90
Row 3 (cream of chicken)	20	56
Creamy Salad Dressing (page 172)*		
Row 1 (cream of asparagus)	23	113
Row 2 (cream of onion)	29	121
Row 3 (cream of mushroom)	28	118
Row 4 (Cheddar cheese)	32	122

*Figures are for 1 tablespoon.

Sweet and Sour Sauce

⅓ cup **Sweetener**
2 tablespoons cornstarch
Spice
1 clove garlic, minced
1 can (10¾ ounces) condensed chicken broth
⅓ cup cider vinegar
1 to 2 teaspoons soy sauce
¼ cup **Vegetable**
Fruit

Sweetener	Spice	Vegetable	Fruit
sugar	¼ teaspoon ground nutmeg	sliced water chestnuts	1 can (8 ounces) mandarin orange segments, drained
honey	6 whole cloves	green onions cut into 1-inch pieces	1 cup pineapple chunks
apple jelly	1 stick cinnamon	zucchini cut into julienne strips	½ cup halved cherry tomatoes
packed brown sugar	⅛ teaspoon minced fresh ginger root	green pepper cut into julienne strips	1 can (8 ounces) apricot halves, drained and cut up

1. In 2-quart saucepan, combine **Sweetener,** cornstarch, **Spice** and garlic. Gradually stir in broth, vinegar and soy sauce. Over medium-high heat, heat to boiling, stirring constantly; boil 1 minute. Discard cloves or cinnamon stick.

2. Stir in **Vegetable** and **Fruit;** heat through. Serve over fish, poultry or meat. Makes about 2 cups.

Shredded Vegetable Sauce

½ cup **Vegetable 1**
Vegetable 2
1 can (10¾ ounces) condensed chicken broth
2 tablespoons cornstarch
½ cup water
Seasoning

Vegetable 1	Vegetable 2	Seasoning
shredded peeled sweet potato	2 green onions, chopped	dash ground allspice
shredded zucchini	¼ cup chopped onion	¼ teaspoon marjoram leaves, crushed
shredded carrot	¼ cup chopped green pepper	1 tablespoon chopped fresh chives

1. In 2-quart saucepan over medium heat, heat **Vegetable 1, Vegetable 2** and chicken broth to simmering.

2. In small bowl, combine cornstarch and water; stir until blended. Stir into simmering soup mixture. Heat to boiling; cook 1 minute more. Add **Seasoning.** Serve over meat, rice or vegetables. Makes about 2 cups.

Souper Gravy

Drippings from roast meat or poultry
1 can (10¾ ounces) condensed **Soup**
Liquid
Seasoning 1
Seasoning 2

Soup	Liquid	Seasoning 1	Seasoning 2
golden mushroom	¼ cup milk	¼ teaspoon tarragon leaves, crushed	1 tablespoon chopped fresh chives
cream of onion	¼ cup water	1 teaspoon Worcestershire	¼ teaspoon marjoram leaves, crushed
cream of chicken	¼ cup sour cream plus ⅓ cup water	½ teaspoon soy sauce	1 tablespoon chopped green onion
cream of celery	2 tablespoons dry sherry plus 2 tablespoons water	⅛ teaspoon ground nutmeg	½ cup cooked or canned sliced mushrooms

1. Remove roast from pan. Pour off pan drippings, reserving 2 tablespoons in pan.

2. Pour **Soup** into roasting pan; stir well to loosen brown bits. Blend in **Liquid.** Add **Seasoning 1** and **Seasoning 2.** Over medium heat, heat through, stirring often. Serve with meat or poultry. Makes about 1½ cups.

Tip: *If you do not have drippings, substitute 2 tablespoons butter or margarine. In 2-quart saucepan over medium heat, melt butter; stir in remaining ingredients. Heat through.*

Golden Mushroom Sauce

2 tablespoons butter or margarine
Vegetable
1 can (10¾ ounces) condensed golden mushroom soup
Liquid
Seasoning

Vegetable	Liquid	Seasoning
2 tablespoons chopped shallots	⅓ cup water plus ¼ cup dry red wine	1 tablespoon chopped fresh parsley
2 tablespoons chopped green onions	⅓ cup water plus ¼ cup dry white wine	⅛ teaspoon basil leaves, crushed, plus 2 tablespoons chopped tomato
¼ cup chopped onion	⅓ cup water plus ¼ cup dry sherry	⅛ teaspoon thyme leaves, crushed
⅓ cup chopped green pepper	½ cup milk	1 tablespoon chopped fresh chives

1. In 2-quart saucepan over medium heat, in hot butter, cook **Vegetable** until tender, stirring occasionally.

2. Stir in soup, **Liquid** and **Seasoning;** heat until boiling, stirring frequently. Serve over beef, lamb or meat loaf. Makes about 2 cups.

To Microwave: In 1-quart microwave-safe casserole, combine butter and **Vegetable;** cover. Microwave on HIGH 1 to 2 minutes until vegetable is tender. Stir in soup, **Liquid** and **Seasoning.** Microwave, uncovered, on HIGH 3 to 5 minutes until boiling, stirring once.

Cream Sauce

1 can (10¾ ounces) condensed **Soup**
Liquid
Flavoring
Seasoning

Soup	Liquid	Flavoring	Seasoning
cream of celery	⅓ cup water plus 2 tablespoons dry sherry	½ cup shredded Swiss cheese	2 tablespoons grated Parmesan cheese
cream of onion	½ cup water	½ cup sour cream	⅛ teaspoon paprika
cream of mushroom	½ cup milk	½ cup cooked or canned sliced mushrooms	2 teaspoons chopped fresh chives
cream of chicken	½ cup light cream	2 tablespoons chopped fresh parsley	¼ teaspoon tarragon leaves, crushed

In 2-quart saucepan, combine all ingredients. Over medium heat, heat through, stirring frequently. Serve over vegetables. Makes about 1½ cups.

To Microwave: In 1-quart microwave-safe casserole, combine all ingredients; cover. Microwave on HIGH 5 to 7 minutes until hot, stirring occasionally.

Blender Hollandaise Sauce

1 can (10¾ ounces) condensed **Soup**
3 egg yolks
2 tablespoons lemon juice
⅛ teaspoon **Seasoning 1**
Dash **Seasoning 2**
½ cup butter or margarine, melted

Soup	Seasoning 1	Seasoning 2
cream of asparagus	hot pepper sauce	freshly ground pepper
cream of chicken	dry mustard	lemon-pepper seasoning
cream of celery	grated lemon peel	cayenne pepper

1. In blender or food processor, combine **Soup,** egg yolks, lemon juice, **Seasoning 1** and **Seasoning 2.** Cover; blend or process until smooth.

2. At high speed, very slowly add butter in a steady stream; blend or process 3 minutes more or until thickened. Serve over vegetables, eggs or fish. Makes about 2 cups.

Cheese Sauce

1 can (10¾ to 11 ounces) condensed **Soup**
Liquid
Cheese
Seasoning

Soup	Liquid	Cheese	Seasoning
cream of celery	⅓ cup milk	1½ cups shredded sharp Cheddar	½ teaspoon dry mustard
cream of mushroom	2 tablespoons sherry plus ⅓ cup milk	1 package (3 ounces) cream cheese, cubed	1 tablespoon Worcestershire
cream of onion	½ cup sour cream plus ⅓ cup milk	½ cup grated Parmesan	1 tablespoon chopped fresh parsley
Cheddar cheese	⅓ cup beer	1½ cups shredded Swiss	dash ground nutmeg

In 2-quart saucepan, combine all ingredients. Over medium heat, heat through, stirring frequently. Serve over vegetables, hamburgers or pasta. Makes about 2 cups.

To Microwave: In 1-quart microwave-safe casserole, combine all ingredients; stir to blend well. Cover. Microwave on HIGH 4 to 6 minutes until hot, stirring occasionally.

Sour Cream Sauce

2 tablespoons butter or margarine
Vegetable
Seasoning
1 can (10¾ ounces) condensed **Soup**
⅓ cup sour cream
⅓ cup milk

Vegetable	Seasoning	Soup
½ cup sliced mushrooms	1 teaspoon Worcestershire	cream of onion
⅓ cup chopped onion	¼ teaspoon paprika	golden mushroom
½ cup chopped celery	¼ teaspoon curry powder	cream of celery
½ cup shredded carrot	¼ teaspoon tarragon leaves, crushed	creamy chicken mushroom

1. In 2-quart saucepan over medium heat, in hot butter, cook **Vegetable** and **Seasoning** until vegetable is tender, stirring occasionally.

2. Stir in **Soup,** sour cream and milk. Heat through, stirring occasionally. Thin to desired consistency with additional milk, if desired. Serve over meat, vegetables, pasta or rice. Makes about 2 cups.

To Microwave: In 1-quart microwave-safe casserole, combine butter, **Vegetable** and **Seasoning;** cover. Microwave on HIGH 2 to 4 minutes until vegetable is tender. Stir in **Soup,** sour cream and milk. Microwave, uncovered, on HIGH 3 to 5 minutes until heated through, stirring occasionally.

Curry Sauce

2 tablespoons butter or margarine
¼ cup chopped onion
2 teaspoons curry powder
1 can (10¾ ounces) condensed **Soup**
½ cup **Liquid**
½ cup **Fruit**
Garnish

Soup	Liquid	Fruit	Garnish
tomato	chicken broth	chopped tomato	raisins
cream of celery	apple juice	chopped apple	salted peanuts
cream of chicken	water	chopped pear	cashews
cream of mushroom	pineapple juice	drained crushed pineapple	toasted flaked coconut

1. In 2-quart saucepan over medium heat, in hot butter, cook onion and curry until onion is tender, stirring occasionally.

2. Stir in **Soup** and **Liquid** until well blended. Add **Fruit;** heat through, stirring occasionally. Top with **Garnish.** Serve over meat, poultry or rice. Makes about 2 cups.

To Microwave: In 1-quart microwave-safe casserole, combine butter, onion and curry; cover. Microwave on HIGH 2 to 3 minutes until onion is tender. Stir in **Soup** and **Liquid** until well blended. Add **Fruit;** cover. Microwave on HIGH 3 to 5 minutes until heated through, stirring occasionally. Top with **Garnish.**

Fruited Barbecue Sauce

2 tablespoons salad oil
½ cup chopped onion
1 clove garlic, minced
1 can (10½ to 10¾ ounces) condensed **Soup**
1 cup **Preserves**
¼ cup **Liquid**
1 tablespoon soy sauce

Soup	Preserves	Liquid
beef broth	apricot preserves	lemon juice
chicken broth	peach preserves	cider vinegar
French onion	orange marmalade	lime juice

1. In 2-quart saucepan over medium heat, in hot oil, cook onion and garlic until tender, stirring occasionally.

2. Stir in remaining ingredients. Reduce heat to low; simmer, uncovered, 15 minutes, stirring occasionally. Use to marinate and baste chicken or ribs. Heat remaining sauce; spoon over meat. Makes about 2 cups.

To Microwave: In 1-quart microwave-safe casserole, combine oil, onion and garlic; cover. Microwave on HIGH 2 to 3 minutes until onion is tender. Stir in remaining ingredients. Microwave, uncovered, on HIGH 4 to 6 minutes until heated through, stirring once.

No-Cook Spicy Barbecue Sauce

1 can (10¾ ounces) condensed tomato soup
Liquid
2 tablespoons **Sweetener**
2 tablespoons Worcestershire
Seasoning
1 teaspoon dry mustard

Liquid	Sweetener	Seasoning
¼ cup cider vinegar	brown sugar	2 teaspoons chili powder
⅓ cup lemon juice	honey	½ teaspoon hot pepper sauce
⅓ cup lime juice	grape jam	2 teaspoons curry powder
¼ cup red wine vinegar	molasses	½ teaspoon ground ginger

In medium bowl, combine all ingredients; stir well. Use to baste chicken, spareribs, lamb, hamburgers or turkey. Makes about 1½ cups.

Chili Sauce

2 tablespoons salad oil
1 medium tomato, chopped
Vegetable
Addition
1 clove garlic, minced
1 can (10¾ ounces) condensed tomato soup
Seasoning
½ teaspoon **Herb,** crushed
1 tablespoon vinegar

Vegetable	Addition	Seasoning	Herb
¼ cup chopped onion	¼ cup chopped green pepper	¼ teaspoon hot pepper sauce	oregano leaves
2 green onions, chopped	⅓ cup chopped celery	2 teaspoons chili powder	basil leaves
¼ cup chopped pitted ripe olives	½ cup salsa	1 tablespoon Worcestershire	marjoram leaves

1. In 2-quart saucepan over medium heat, in hot oil, cook tomato, **Vegetable, Addition** and garlic until vegetables are tender, stirring occasionally.

2. Stir in soup, **Seasoning, Herb** and vinegar. Heat to boiling, stirring occasionally. Reduce heat to low; simmer, uncovered, 10 minutes, stirring occasionally. Serve over fish, hamburgers or frankfurters, or stir into cooked rice. Makes about 2 cups.

To Microwave: In 1-quart microwave-safe casserole, combine oil, tomato, **Vegetable, Addition** and garlic; cover. Microwave on HIGH 2 to 4 minutes until vegetables are tender, stirring once. Stir in soup, **Seasoning, Herb** and vinegar; cover. Microwave on HIGH 2 to 4 minutes until boiling, stirring once.

Eggplant Pasta Sauce

½ cup salad oil
1 eggplant (1 pound), cut into 1-inch cubes
1 cup chopped onion
Vegetable
1 clove garlic, minced
1 can (10½ to 11 ounces) condensed **Soup**
Tomatoes
Seasoning
1 bay leaf
6 drops hot pepper sauce

Vegetable	Soup	Tomatoes	Seasoning
1 cup sliced mushrooms	tomato bisque	1 can (28 ounces) tomatoes, cut up (do not drain)	1 teaspoon oregano leaves plus ½ teaspoon thyme leaves, crushed
½ cup chopped green pepper	tomato	2 cans (15 ounces each) tomato sauce	2 teaspoons basil leaves, crushed
¼ cup chopped parsley	Spanish style vegetable	1 can (12 ounces) tomato paste plus 2 cups water	2 teaspoons chili powder plus 1 teaspoon ground cumin

1. In 4-quart Dutch oven over medium heat, in hot oil, cook eggplant, onion, **Vegetable** and garlic about 10 minutes, stirring frequently.

2. Add remaining ingredients; heat to boiling. Reduce heat to low. Simmer, uncovered, 45 minutes or until desired consistency, stirring occasionally. Discard bay leaf. Serve over hot pasta. Makes about 6 cups, 6 servings.

Carbonara Sauce

1 can (10¾ ounces) condensed **Soup**
Meat
Flavoring
½ cup half-and-half
Cheese

Soup	Meat	Flavoring	Cheese
cream of onion	6 slices bacon, cooked, drained and crumbled	¼ cup chopped parsley	2 tablespoons grated Romano
cream of celery	½ pound bulk pork sausage, cooked, drained and crumbled	2 tablespoons chopped green onions	2 tablespoons grated Parmesan
cream of shrimp	1 cup diced cooked ham	¼ cup chopped green pepper	¼ cup grated Gruyère
cream of mushroom	½ cup diced prosciutto	2 tablespoons chopped fresh basil leaves	½ cup shredded Swiss

1. In 2-quart saucepan over medium heat, heat **Soup, Meat, Flavoring** and half-and-half until hot, stirring frequently.

2. Stir in **Cheese** until melted. Serve over hot cooked pasta. Makes about 2 cups, 4 servings.

To Microwave: In 1-quart microwave-safe casserole, combine **Soup, Meat, Flavoring** and half-and-half; cover. Microwave on HIGH 4 to 6 minutes until hot, stirring once. Stir in **Cheese** until melted.

CALORIE AND SODIUM GUIDE (PER SERVING)

Recipe	Calories	Sodium (mg)
Sweet and Sour Sauce (page 174)*		
Row 1 (sugar)	20	141
Row 2 (honey)	20	140
Row 3 (apple jelly)	14	140
Row 4 (brown sugar)	15	140
Shredded Vegetable Sauce (page 176)*		
Row 1 (sweet potato)	8	75
Row 2 (zucchini)	5	75
Row 3 (carrot)	5	76
Souper Gravy (page 177)*		
Row 1 (golden mushroom)	22	113
Row 2 (cream of onion)	22	122
Row 3 (cream of chicken)	27	126
Row 4 (cream of celery)	23	118
Golden Mushroom Sauce (page 178)*		
Row 1 (shallots)	15	92
Row 2 (green onions)	15	92
Row 3 (onion)	17	92
Row 4 (green pepper)	16	94
Cream Sauce (page 179)*		
Row 1 (cream of celery)	24	122
Row 2 (cream of onion)	22	105
Row 3 (cream of mushroom)	17	109
Row 4 (cream of chicken)	21	109
Blender Hollandaise Sauce (page 180)*		
Row 1 (cream of asparagus)	39	114
Row 2 (cream of chicken)	42	110
Row 3 (cream of celery)	41	111
Cheese Sauce (page 182)*		
Row 1 (cream of celery)	32	115
Row 2 (cream of mushroom)	23	90
Row 3 (cream of onion)	24	109
Row 4 (Cheddar cheese)	33	98

Recipe	Calories	Sodium (mg)
Sour Cream Sauce (page 183)*		
Row 1 (mushrooms)	23	94
Row 2 (onion)	23	87
Row 3 (celery)	22	93
Row 4 (carrot)	24	98
Curry Sauce (page 184)*		
Row 1 (tomato)	21	86
Row 2 (cream of celery)	24	88
Row 3 (cream of chicken)	24	87
Row 4 (cream of mushroom)	22	85
Fruited Barbecue Sauce (page 185)*		
Row 1 (beef broth)	38	90
Row 2 (chicken broth)	39	107
Row 3 (French onion)	41	121
No-Cook Spicy Barbecue Sauce (page 187)*		
Row 1 (cider vinegar)	21	104
Row 2 (lemon juice)	21	102
Row 3 (lime juice)	21	102
Row 4 (red wine vinegar)	19	102
Chili Sauce (page 188)*		
Row 1 (onion)	17	70
Row 2 (green onions)	18	73
Row 3 (olives)	24	131
Eggplant Pasta Sauce (page 189)		
Row 1 (mushrooms)	277	619
Row 2 (green pepper)	307	1035
Row 3 (parsley)	273	689
Carbonara Sauce (page 190)		
Row 1 (cream of onion)	192	832
Row 2 (cream of celery)	248	960
Row 3 (cream of shrimp)	200	1024
Row 4 (cream of mushroom)	216	1200

*Figures are for 1 tablespoon.

Sandwiches and Breads

Cheese Plus Sandwiches

1 package (3 ounces) cream cheese, softened
1 can (11 ounces) condensed Cheddar cheese soup
Seasoning
Bread
Lettuce leaves
Sliced tomato
Protein
Garnish

Seasoning	Bread	Protein	Garnish
1 tablespoon prepared horseradish	8 slices pumpernickel	2 cans (3¾ ounces each) sardines, drained	red onion rings
1 tablespoon prepared mustard	8 slices rye	8 slices cooked ham	dill pickle slices
1 tablespoon finely chopped jalapeño peppers	4 pita rounds, halved	1 can (16 ounces) red kidney beans, drained	diced avocado
¼ teaspoon ground ginger	8 slices whole wheat	8 slices cooked turkey	sliced peaches

1. In small bowl with mixer at medium speed, beat cream cheese until smooth. Beat in soup and **Seasoning** until well mixed.

2. Spread cheese mixture evenly onto one side of each **Bread** slice (or spread inside of pita bread). Top with lettuce, tomato, **Protein** and **Garnish.** Makes 8 servings.

Cheese-Topped Sandwich Stacks

4 English muffins, split and toasted
8 slices bacon, halved, cooked and drained
1⅓ cups **Vegetable 1**
8 ounces **Meat**
Vegetable 2
1 can (10¾ to 11 ounces) condensed **Soup**
¼ cup milk
1½ cups shredded Cheddar cheese
1 tablespoon Worcestershire
½ teaspoon dry mustard

Vegetable 1	Meat	Vegetable 2	Soup
shredded lettuce	thinly sliced cooked ham	8 slices tomato	cream of mushroom
bean sprouts	thinly sliced cooked turkey	1 avocado, sliced	cream of chicken
alfalfa sprouts	thinly sliced roast beef	hot pickled peppers	Cheddar cheese

1. Place toasted English muffins on baking sheet. Top each half with bacon, **Vegetable 1, Meat** and **Vegetable 2.** Set aside.

2. In 2-quart saucepan, combine **Soup** and milk. Over medium heat, heat through, stirring occasionally. Add cheese, Worcestershire and dry mustard. Heat until cheese melts, stirring constantly. Pour sauce over each muffin.

3. Broil 4 inches from heat 1 to 2 minutes until tops start to brown. Makes 4 servings.

Spread-a-Burger

1 can (10¾ to 11 ounces) condensed **Soup**
1½ pounds **Meat**
Seasoning
⅓ cup chopped onion
⅛ teaspoon pepper
8 long hard rolls, split
2 cups shredded **Cheese**

Soup	Meat	Seasoning	Cheese
Cheddar cheese	bulk pork sausage	½ teaspoon celery seed	mozzarella
tomato	ground beef	1 tablespoon Worcestershire	Cheddar
cream of mushroom	ground pork	1 tablespoon prepared horseradish	Swiss
golden mushroom	ground lamb	1 tablespoon prepared mustard	American

1. In large bowl, blend **Soup, Meat, Seasoning,** onion and pepper until thoroughly mixed. Spread ¼ cup meat mixture evenly on each roll half, spreading to cover edges.

2. Place rolls meat side up on baking sheet. Broil 4 to 6 inches from heat 7 to 8 minutes until meat is done.

3. Sprinkle rolls with **Cheese;** broil until cheese melts. Makes 8 servings.

Sausage-Vegetable Rolls

½ pound bulk pork sausage
1 cup chopped onion
1 cup **Vegetable**
1 can (10½ to 11 ounces) condensed **Soup**
1 loaf (1 pound) frozen bread dough, thawed
½ cup **Cheese**
1 egg, beaten
1 tablespoon **Topping**

Vegetable	Soup	Cheese	Topping
frozen chopped broccoli, thawed and drained	golden mushroom	grated Romano	sesame seed
sauerkraut, rinsed and drained	cream of celery	shredded Swiss	wheat germ
frozen chopped spinach, thawed and drained	Cheddar cheese	shredded Cheddar	poppy seed

1. Preheat oven to 350°F. Grease large baking sheet.

2. In 10-inch skillet over medium heat, cook sausage until it begins to brown, stirring to break up meat. Add onion and **Vegetable;** cook about 5 minutes until meat is browned and vegetables are tender, stirring occasionally. Pour off fat. Stir in **Soup.** Cool to room temperature.

3. Divide thawed dough into 6 equal parts. On floured surface, roll out 1 part to a 6-inch round. Place about ½ cup sausage mixture on dough, spreading to within 1 inch of edges. Sprinkle with 1 generous tablespoon of the **Cheese.** Fold over to form a half circle. Pinch edges to seal. Place on prepared baking sheet. Repeat with remaining dough.

4. Brush rolls with egg; sprinkle with **Topping.** Bake 25 minutes or until golden brown. Let stand 10 minutes. Serve warm. Makes 6 servings.

Barbecued Beef Sandwiches

1 pound ground beef
½ cup chopped onion
½ cup chopped green pepper
1 clove garlic, minced
1 can (10½ to 11¼ ounces) condensed **Soup**
1 can (10¾ ounces) condensed tomato soup
2 tablespoons vinegar
Seasoning
¼ teaspoon pepper
Bread, split and toasted

Soup	Seasoning	Bread
Spanish style vegetable	1 teaspoon dry mustard	8 hamburger buns
golden mushroom	¼ teaspoon hot pepper sauce	8 English muffins
vegetarian vegetable	1 tablespoon chopped jalapeño pepper	8 frankfurter buns
chili beef plus ¼ cup water	1 teaspoon chili powder	8 hard rolls

1. In 10-inch skillet over medium heat, cook ground beef, onion, green pepper and garlic until meat is browned and vegetables are tender, stirring often to break up meat. Pour off fat.

2. Stir in **Soup,** tomato soup, vinegar, **Seasoning** and pepper. Heat to boiling, stirring occasionally. Reduce heat to low. Simmer, uncovered, 20 minutes or until desired consistency. Serve in or over **Bread,** using about ⅓ cup per serving. Makes 8 servings.

To Microwave: In 2-quart microwave-safe casserole, crumble beef. Add onion, green pepper and garlic; cover. Microwave on HIGH 6 to 8 minutes until meat is browned and vegetables are tender, stirring occasionally. Pour off fat. Stir in **Soup,** tomato soup, vinegar, **Seasoning** and pepper; cover. Microwave on HIGH 7 to 9 minutes until boiling, stirring occasionally. Serve as in Step 2.

Scrambled Eggs in Pita Pockets

4 pita bread rounds, halved
8 eggs
1 can (10¾ ounces) condensed **Soup**
1 cup **Vegetable**
Meat
2 tablespoons butter or margarine
1 cup shredded **Cheese**

Soup	Vegetable	Meat	Cheese
cream of mushroom	sliced mushrooms	6 slices bacon, diced	Cheddar
cream of celery	diced tomatoes	1 cup diced cooked ham plus 2 tablespoons salad oil	American
cream of chicken	chopped green pepper	¼ pound bulk pork sausage	Monterey Jack
cream of onion	diced zucchini	¼ pound pepperoni, diced	Muenster

1. Wrap pita bread in aluminum foil; bake at 350°F. 15 minutes or until warm.

2. Meanwhile, in bowl with whisk or rotary beater, beat eggs until foamy. Stir in **Soup** and **Vegetable;** set aside.

3. In 10-inch skillet over medium heat, cook bacon or pork sausage until done, or cook ham or pepperoni until heated through, stirring occasionally. Pour off fat.

4. Add butter to skillet; heat until foamy. Add egg mixture; cook until set but still slightly moist, stirring and lifting eggs so uncooked portion flows to bottom.

5. Stuff warm pita pockets with egg mixture. Add **Cheese** to each. Makes 8 servings.

Sausage Breakfast Bake

12 ounces **Sausage**
2 tablespoons water
1 can (10¾ to 11 ounces) condensed **Soup**
2 eggs
¾ cup **Liquid**
2 tablespoons salad oil
1 cup all-purpose flour
1 cup cornmeal
¼ cup sugar
1 tablespoon baking powder
Butter or margarine
Topping

Sausage	Soup	Liquid	Topping
pork sausage links	cream of mushroom	apple juice	honey
smoked sausage links	Cheddar cheese	milk	maple syrup
Italian sausage in casings, cut into 2-inch lengths	cream of celery	chicken broth	fruit preserves

1. Preheat oven to 350°F. Grease 12 by 8-inch baking dish.

2. In covered 10-inch skillet over medium heat, cook **Sausage** in water 5 minutes. Uncover; cook until sausages are browned, turning occasionally. Drain on paper towels.

3. In small bowl, combine **Soup** and eggs; stir to mix well. Gradually stir in **Liquid** and oil; mix until smooth.

4. In medium bowl, combine flour, cornmeal, sugar and baking powder. Add soup mixture, stirring just to moisten. Pour into prepared baking dish. Arrange sausages on batter.

5. Bake 30 minutes or until bread springs back when lightly touched with finger. Serve warm with butter and **Topping.** Makes 6 servings.

Potato Doughnuts

Flour
1 cup sugar
2 packages active dry yeast
1 can (10¾ ounces) condensed cream of potato soup
1 soup can **Liquid**
¼ cup butter or margarine
Flavoring
1 egg
Salad oil
Coating

Flour	Liquid	Flavoring	Coating
6 to 6½ cups all-purpose	water	¼ teaspoon ground nutmeg	cinnamon/sugar
2 cups whole wheat plus 4 to 4½ cups all-purpose	milk	½ teaspoon grated lemon peel	confectioners' sugar
½ cup wheat germ plus 5½ to 6 cups all-purpose	orange juice	1 teaspoon grated orange peel	glaze (see **Tip** below)

1. In large bowl, stir together 3 cups of the **Flour,** sugar and yeast. In blender or food processor, blend soup until smooth. In 2-quart saucepan over low heat, heat soup, **Liquid,** butter and **Flavoring** until mixture is very warm (120° to 130°F.). Butter does not need to melt completely.

2. With mixer at low speed, gradually pour soup mixture into dry ingredients. At medium speed, beat 2 minutes, scraping bowl with rubber spatula. Beat in egg and ½ cup of the **Flour;** beat 2 minutes more, scraping bowl occasionally. With spoon, stir in enough additional **Flour** (about 2½ cups) to make a soft dough. On floured surface, knead until smooth and elastic, about 10 minutes.

3. Shape dough into ball; place in greased large bowl, turning dough over to grease top. Cover; let rise in warm place until doubled, about 1 hour.

4. Punch dough down by pushing center of dough with fist, then pushing edges of dough to center. On floured surface, roll out dough to ¼ inch thickness; cut with floured 3-inch doughnut cutter. Cover; let rise until doubled, about 30 minutes.

5. In skillet or Dutch oven, heat 1 inch oil to 375°F. Fry doughnuts, a few at a time, in hot oil until browned, about 1 minute on each side. Drain on paper towels. Cover warm doughnuts with **Coating.** Makes about 30 doughnuts.

Tip: *To make glaze, in medium bowl, combine 1 pound confectioners' sugar, 6 tablespoons water or orange juice and 1 tablespoon vanilla. Dip doughnuts in glaze to coat on both sides.*

Double Cheese Ring

Flour
2 tablespoons sugar
4 teaspoons baking powder
¾ cup shortening
1 can (11 ounces) condensed Cheddar cheese soup
¼ cup milk
4 ounces **Cheese,** thinly sliced
1 egg yolk
2 teaspoons water
Topping

Flour	Cheese	Topping
1 cup whole wheat plus 2 cups all-purpose	American	poppy seed
3 cups all-purpose	Cheddar	sesame seed
½ cup rye plus 2½ cups all-purpose	Swiss	caraway seed
½ cup wheat germ plus 2½ cups all-purpose	Monterey Jack	minced dried onion

1. Preheat oven to 425°F. Grease large baking sheet.

2. In large bowl, stir together **Flour,** sugar and baking powder. With pastry blender, cut in shortening until mixture resembles coarse crumbs.

3. In small bowl, combine soup and milk; mix well. Add to flour mixture, stirring with fork just until dough forms. Turn out onto lightly floured surface. Knead dough 10 times. Divide dough in half.

4. Roll out each dough half to 12-inch circle. Cut each into 8 wedges. Cut sliced **Cheese** into 16 pieces, if necessary. Place 1 piece of the cheese on each dough wedge. Roll up jelly-roll fashion from outside edge. On prepared baking sheet, arrange rolls side-by-side to form a ring.

5. In small bowl, combine egg yolk and water; brush on ring. Sprinkle with **Topping.**

6. Bake 25 to 30 minutes until browned. Serve warm. Makes 16 servings.

No-Knead Onion Bread

Flour
2 tablespoons sugar
2 packages active dry yeast
1 can (10½ ounces) condensed French onion soup
¼ cup butter or margarine
1 egg
1 cup **Cheese**
1 tablespoon water
2 teaspoons **Topping**

Flour	Cheese	Topping
3 cups all-purpose	grated Romano	sesame seed
1 cup rye plus 2 cups all-purpose	shredded Cheddar	poppy seed
1½ cups whole wheat plus 1½ cups all-purpose	shredded American	minced dried onion

1. In large bowl, combine 1 cup of the **Flour,** sugar and yeast.

2. In small saucepan over medium heat, heat soup and butter until very warm (120° to 130°F.). Butter does not need to melt completely.

3. With mixer at low speed, gradually pour soup mixture into dry ingredients, mixing well. At medium speed, beat 3 minutes or until smooth. Add egg, **Cheese** and 1 cup of the **Flour;** beat 2 minutes more.

4. With spoon, stir in enough remaining **Flour** to make a stiff batter. Cover; let rise in warm place until doubled, about 1½ hours.

5. Grease 1½-quart casserole. Stir down batter. Turn into casserole. Cover; let rise until doubled, about 45 minutes. Preheat oven to 325°F.

6. Brush with water and sprinkle with **Topping.** Bake 50 minutes or until bread sounds hollow when tapped with finger. Remove from pan; cool on wire rack before slicing. Makes 1 loaf, 16 servings.

Tip: *When using a mixture of flours, stir flours together well before using. If you need any additional flour, use all-purpose.*

German Cheese Fruit Kuchen

3½ to 3¾ cups all-purpose flour
¼ cup sugar
2 packages active dry yeast
1 can (11 ounces) condensed Cheddar cheese soup
½ cup water
¼ cup butter or margarine
4 eggs
Filling
1 package (8 ounces) cream cheese, softened
⅓ cup sugar
Flavoring 1
Flavoring 2
Topping

Filling	Flavoring 1	Flavoring 2	Topping
1 can (21 ounces) cherry pie filling	1 tablespoon grated orange peel	2 tablespoons orange juice	ground nutmeg
4 cups shredded apples tossed with ¼ cup additional sugar	2 teaspoons grated lemon peel	2 tablespoons lemon juice	vanilla wafer crumbs
1 can (21 ounces) blueberry pie filling	2 teaspoons vanilla extract	1 teaspoon ground cinnamon	gingersnap crumbs
1 can (20 ounces) crushed pineapple, drained	¼ teaspoon almond extract	2 tablespoons orange liqueur	toasted flaked coconut

1. In large bowl, stir together 1½ cups of the flour, ¼ cup sugar and yeast. In 1-quart saucepan over low heat, heat ½ cup of the soup, water and butter until mixture is very warm (120° to 130°F.). Butter does not need to melt completely.

2. With mixer at low speed, gradually pour soup mixture into dry ingredients. At medium speed, beat 2 minutes, scraping bowl with rubber spatula. Beat in 2 of the eggs and ½ cup of the flour; beat 2 minutes more, scraping bowl occasionally. With spoon, stir in enough additional flour (about 1½ cups) to make a soft dough. On floured surface, knead until smooth and elastic, about 5 minutes. Shape dough into ball; place in greased large bowl, turning to grease top. Cover; let rise in warm place until doubled, about 45 minutes.

3. Grease 13 by 9-inch baking pan. Press dough into prepared pan, making 1-inch rim on edges. Top with **Filling.** Cover and let rise until doubled, about 30 minutes. Preheat oven to 350°F.

4. Meanwhile, in small bowl with mixer at medium speed, beat cream cheese and remaining soup until smooth. Beat in remaining 2 eggs and ⅓ cup sugar. Stir in **Flavoring 1** and **Flavoring 2;** pour over filling. Sprinkle with **Topping.**

5. Bake 45 to 55 minutes until crust is golden brown and cheese is set. Cool slightly in pan on rack. Serve warm. Makes 12 servings.

Giant Zucchini Muffins

2½ cups all-purpose flour
Addition
⅓ cup sugar
1 tablespoon baking powder
Herb, crushed
1 can (10¾ ounces) condensed **Soup**
½ cup **Liquid**
2 eggs
¼ cup salad oil
1 cup shredded zucchini

Addition	Herb	Soup	Liquid
½ cup quick-cooking oats	1 teaspoon dill weed	cream of asparagus	milk
½ cup wheat germ	1 teaspoon summer savory leaves	cream of celery	orange juice
½ cup finely chopped nuts	½ teaspoon thyme leaves	cream of mushroom	water

1. Preheat oven to 400°F. Grease twelve 3-inch muffin-pan cups.

2. In large bowl, combine flour, **Addition,** sugar, baking powder and **Herb.**

3. In medium bowl, combine **Soup, Liquid,** eggs, oil and zucchini; mix well. Add to dry ingredients, stirring just to moisten. (Batter will be lumpy.)

4. Spoon batter into muffin cups, filling almost full. Bake 25 minutes or until toothpick inserted in center of muffin comes out clean. Serve warm. Makes 12 muffins.

Tea Bread

1 can (10¾ to 11 ounces) condensed **Soup**
½ cup sugar
¼ cup packed brown sugar
2 tablespoons salad oil
1 egg, beaten
2 cups all-purpose flour
2 teaspoons baking powder
Flavoring
1 cup **Addition 1**
½ cup **Addition 2**

Soup	Flavoring	Addition 1	Addition 2
Cheddar cheese	2 teaspoons grated orange peel	chopped cranberries	chopped walnuts
cream of celery	1 teaspoon grated lemon peel	chopped dried apricots	toasted flaked coconut
cream of mushroom	1 teaspoon ground cinnamon	shredded carrots	raisins

1. Preheat oven to 350°F. Grease 9 by 5-inch loaf pan.

2. In medium bowl, stir together **Soup,** sugar, brown sugar, oil and egg; mix until blended.

3. Add flour, baking powder and **Flavoring;** stir just until moistened. Stir in **Addition 1** and **Addition 2.**

4. Turn batter into prepared pan. Bake 1 hour 10 minutes or until toothpick inserted in center comes out clean. Cool in pan on rack 10 minutes. Remove from pan; cool on rack. Makes 1 loaf, 16 servings.

CALORIE AND SODIUM GUIDE (PER SERVING)

Recipe	Calories	Sodium (mg)
Cheese Plus Sandwiches (page 192)		
Row 1 (horseradish)	260	946
Row 2 (mustard)	182	716
Row 3 (jalapeño peppers)	229	533
Row 4 (ginger)	186	638
Cheese-Topped Sandwich Stacks (page 194)		
Row 1 (lettuce)	530	1307
Row 2 (bean sprouts)	519	1346
Row 3 (alfalfa sprouts)	574	1369
Spread-a-Burger (page 195)		
Row 1 (Cheddar cheese)	709	1609
Row 2 (tomato)	639	1293
Row 3 (cream of mushroom)	748	1197
Row 4 (golden mushroom)	637	1463
Sausage-Vegetable Rolls (page 197)		
Row 1 (broccoli)	434	1258
Row 2 (sauerkraut)	408	1426
Row 3 (spinach)	433	1197
Barbecued Beef Sandwiches (page 198)		
Row 1 (Spanish style vegetable)	290	710
Row 2 (golden mushroom)	170	914
Row 3 (vegetarian vegetable)	249	340
Row 4 (chili beef)	235	700
Scrambled Eggs in Pita Pockets (page 199)		
Row 1 (cream of mushroom)	327	707
Row 2 (cream of celery)	354	792
Row 3 (cream of chicken)	326	712
Row 4 (cream of onion)	360	940
Sausage Breakfast Bake (page 200)		
Row 1 (pork sausage links)	519	1250
Row 2 (smoked sausage links)	830	1853
Row 3 (Italian sausage)	501	1773

Recipe	Calories	Sodium (mg)
Potato Doughnuts (page 202)		
Row 1 (all-purpose)	177	105
Row 2 (whole wheat plus all-purpose)	183	111
Row 3 (wheat germ plus all-purpose)	180	105
Double Cheese Ring (page 203)		
Row 1 (whole wheat plus all-purpose)	244	376
Row 2 (all-purpose)	226	317
Row 3 (rye plus all-purpose)	225	293
Row 4 (wheat germ plus all-purpose)	220	313
No-Knead Onion Bread (page 205)		
Row 1 (all-purpose)	155	294
Row 2 (rye plus all-purpose)	154	252
Row 3 (whole wheat plus all-purpose)	152	310
German Cheese Fruit Kuchen (page 206)		
Row 1 (cherry pie filling)	397	352
Row 2 (apples with sugar)	403	438
Row 3 (blueberry pie filling)	364	296
Row 4 (pineapple)	370	351
Giant Zucchini Muffins (page 207)		
Row 1 (quick-cooking oats)	198	344
Row 2 (wheat germ)	203	327
Row 3 (nuts)	215	316
Tea Bread (page 208)		
Row 1 (Cheddar cheese)	158	228
Row 2 (cream of celery)	164	232
Row 3 (cream of mushroom)	146	213

Desserts

Saucepan Brownies

½ cup butter or margarine
Flavoring
1 can (11 ounces) condensed Cheddar cheese soup
½ cup **Sweetener**
2 eggs, beaten
1½ cups all-purpose flour
2 teaspoons baking powder
1 cup **Addition**

Flavoring	Sweetener	Addition
1 package (12 ounces) semisweet-chocolate pieces	sugar	chopped pecans
1 package (12 ounces) butterscotch-flavor pieces (use only ¼ cup butter)	packed brown sugar	flaked coconut
12 ounces white chocolate, broken into chunks	light corn syrup	pistachio nuts

1. Preheat oven to 350°F. Grease 13 by 9-inch baking pan.

2. In 3-quart saucepan over medium heat, melt butter. Reduce heat to low. Add **Flavoring;** stir until melted. Remove from heat.

3. With spoon, beat in soup, **Sweetener** and eggs. Add flour and baking powder; stir until blended. Stir in ¾ cup of the **Addition.** Spread batter in prepared pan. Sprinkle with remaining ¼ cup **Addition.**

4. Bake 25 to 35 minutes until top springs back when lightly touched. Cool in pan on rack. Makes 24 brownies.

Fruited Spice Cake Squares

1 package (2-layer size) spice cake mix
1 can (10¾ ounces) condensed tomato soup
½ cup water
2 eggs
1 cup **Fruit**
½ cup butter or margarine, softened
3 cups confectioners' sugar
1 teaspoon **Flavoring**
3 tablespoons **Liquid**
1 cup **Topping**

Fruit	Flavoring	Liquid	Topping
raisins	grated orange peel	orange juice	finely chopped walnuts
chopped dried apricots	vanilla extract	milk	granola
chopped prunes	grated lemon peel	apple juice	toasted flaked coconut

1. Preheat oven to 350°F. Grease 15 by 10-inch jelly-roll pan.

2. Mix cake mix, tomato soup, water and eggs, following directions on package. Fold in **Fruit.** Pour batter into prepared pan.

3. Bake 25 to 30 minutes until toothpick inserted in cake comes out clean. Cool completely in pan on wire rack.

4. In medium bowl, beat butter until creamy. Gradually add confectioners' sugar, **Flavoring** and **Liquid,** stirring until smooth. Spread on cake; sprinkle with **Topping.** Cut cake into squares. Makes 24 squares.

Three-Fruit Cake Squares

2 cups all-purpose flour
1 teaspoon baking powder
½ teaspoon baking soda
Ground **Spice**
½ cup butter or margarine
1½ cups sugar
2 eggs
1 can (10¾ ounces) condensed tomato soup
Flavoring
½ cup chopped apple
½ cup **Fruit**
½ cup **Dried Fruit**
Confectioners' sugar

Spice	Flavoring	Fruit	Dried Fruit
1 teaspoon nutmeg	1 teaspoon grated lemon peel	chopped fresh or frozen cranberries	chopped dried apricots
1 teaspoon cinnamon	½ teaspoon almond extract	drained crushed pineapple	raisins
½ teaspoon allspice plus ½ teaspoon ginger	1 teaspoon vanilla extract	fresh or frozen blueberries	chopped dried figs

1. Preheat oven to 350°F. Grease and flour 13 by 9-inch baking pan.

2. Stir together flour, baking powder, baking soda and **Spice;** set aside.

3. In large bowl with mixer at medium speed, cream together butter and sugar until light and fluffy. Beat in eggs, one at a time, beating well after each addition. Add soup and **Flavoring** alternately with flour mixture, beating 1 minute after each addition.

4. Stir in apple, **Fruit** and **Dried Fruit** just until mixed. Pour into prepared pan. Bake 40 minutes or until toothpick inserted in cake comes out clean. Cool in pan on rack. Dust with confectioners' sugar. Makes 15 servings.

Souper Cheesecake

1 cup **Crumbs**
¼ cup butter or margarine, melted
12 ounces cream cheese, softened
⅔ cup sugar
3 eggs
1 can (11 ounces) condensed Cheddar cheese soup
Flavoring 1
Flavoring 2
Topping

Crumbs	Flavoring 1	Flavoring 2	Topping
graham cracker	1 teaspoon grated lemon peel	2 tablespoons lemon juice	fresh strawberries
zwieback	2 teaspoons grated orange peel	2 tablespoons orange juice	fresh blueberries
gingersnap	1 teaspoon pumpkin pie spice	2 teaspoons vanilla extract	canned cherry pie filling
vanilla wafer	3 ounces semisweet chocolate, melted	2 tablespoons coffee liqueur	sweetened whipped cream

1. In small bowl, combine **Crumbs** and butter; mix well. Press crumb mixture into bottom of 9-inch springform pan to make an even layer. Set aside.

2. In large bowl with mixer at medium speed, beat cream cheese until smooth. Alternately add sugar and eggs, beating well after each addition. Beat in soup, **Flavoring 1** and **Flavoring 2** until blended. Pour over crust.

3. Bake at 350°F. 1 hour or until puffed around edges and set in center. Cool completely in pan on wire rack. Refrigerate until serving time, at least 4 hours. Garnish with **Topping.** Makes 12 servings.

Spicy Vegetable Cake

2 cups all-purpose flour
1⅓ cups packed brown sugar
2 teaspoons baking powder
1 teaspoon baking soda
Ground **Spice**
1 can (10¾ ounces) condensed tomato soup
½ cup shortening
2 eggs
¼ cup **Syrup**
1 cup shredded **Vegetable**
½ cup **Addition**

Spice	Syrup	Vegetable	Addition
1 teaspoon allspice plus 1 teaspoon nutmeg plus 1 teaspoon cinnamon	molasses	carrots	raisins
1½ teaspoons ginger plus ½ teaspoon cloves plus ½ teaspoon cinnamon	honey	zucchini	flaked coconut
1 tablespoon pumpkin pie spice	maple-flavored syrup	peeled sweet potatoes	chopped nuts

1. Preheat oven to 350°F. Grease 10-inch tube pan.

2. In large bowl, combine flour, brown sugar, baking powder, baking soda and **Spice.** Add soup and shortening. With mixer at medium speed, beat 2 minutes, constantly scraping sides and bottom of bowl.

3. Add eggs and **Syrup;** beat 2 minutes more. Fold in **Vegetable** and **Addition.** Turn into prepared pan; bake about 1 hour until toothpick inserted in cake comes out clean. Cool in pan on rack 10 minutes. Remove from pan; cool completely. Serve plain or topped with whipped cream. Makes 16 servings.

Tip: *This cake can be baked in a greased and floured 13 by 9-inch baking pan at 350°F. 40 to 50 minutes.*

Rice Pudding

1 can (11 ounces) condensed Cheddar cheese soup
4 cups milk
½ cup **Sweetener**
Flavoring
Ground **Spice**
⅓ cup raw regular rice
Addition

Sweetener	Flavoring	Spice	Addition
sugar	2 teaspoons vanilla extract	½ teaspoon cinnamon	½ cup raisins
honey	½ teaspoon grated lemon peel	dash cloves	1 can (8 ounces) crushed pineapple, drained, plus ¼ cup flaked coconut
packed brown sugar	1 teaspoon vanilla extract plus ½ teaspoon almond extract	¼ teaspoon nutmeg	½ cup chopped dates
molasses	1 teaspoon grated orange peel	¼ teaspoon ginger	½ cup chopped dried figs

1. In 4-quart saucepan, stir together soup, milk, **Sweetener, Flavoring** and **Spice.** Over medium heat, heat to boiling, stirring constantly. Stir in rice.

2. Reduce heat to low. Simmer, uncovered, 1 hour or until rice is very tender and mixture is thickened, stirring occasionally. Stir in **Addition.** Pour into dessert dishes. Refrigerate until serving time, at least 4 hours. Makes about 4 cups, 6 servings.

CALORIE AND SODIUM GUIDE (PER SERVING)

Recipe	Calories	Sodium (mg)
Saucepan Brownies (page 210)		
Row 1 (semisweet-chocolate pieces)	206	212
Row 2 (butterscotch-flavor pieces)	172	193
Row 3 (white chocolate)	207	216
Fruited Spice Cake Squares (page 212)		
Row 1 (raisins)	291	266
Row 2 (apricots)	281	275
Row 3 (prunes)	276	265
Three-Fruit Cake Squares (page 213)		
Row 1 (nutmeg)	242	288
Row 2 (cinnamon)	249	289
Row 3 (allspice plus ginger)	247	288

Recipe	Calories	Sodium (mg)
Souper Cheesecake (page 215)		
Row 1 (graham cracker)	269	425
Row 2 (zwieback)	293	384
Row 3 (gingersnap)	348	491
Row 4 (vanilla wafer)	301	387
Spicy Vegetable Cake (page 216)		
Row 1 (allspice plus nutmeg plus cinnamon)	233	300
Row 2 (ginger plus cloves plus cinnamon)	231	274
Row 3 (pumpkin pie spice)	255	278
Rice Pudding (page 217)		
Row 1 (sugar)	282	544
Row 2 (honey)	298	544
Row 3 (brown sugar)	291	549
Row 4 (molasses)	278	553

Index